Sexual Harassment: Issues and Analyses

Sexual Harassment: Issues and Analyses

Janet V. Lewis (Editor)

Nova Science Publishers, Inc.
Huntington, NY

Senior Editor: Susan Boriotti
Office Manager: Annette Hellinger
Graphics: Wanda Serrano
Information Editor: Tatiana Shohov
Book Production: Cathy DeGregory, Kay Seymour and Jennifer Vogt
Circulation: Ave Maria Gonzalez, Mike Hedges, Ron Hedges and Andre Tillman

Library of Congress Cataloging-in-Publication Data
Available Upon Request

ISBN 1-56072-955-4.

227 Main Street, Suite 100
Huntington, New York 11743
Tele. 631-424-6682 Fax 631-424-4666
E Mail Novascil@aol.com

Printed in the United States of America

CONTENTS

CIVIL RIGHTS AND CRIMINAL JUSTICE: PRIMER ON SEXUAL HARASSMENT

*Paula N. Rubin**

HIGHLIGHTS

This Research in Action, the seventh in a series that examines civil rights laws as they affect the criminal justice community, takes a close look at sexual harassment--a form of sexual discrimination that is in the forefront of the American consciousness. Although the issue of sexual harassment is one that touches all employers, its relevance to law enforcement agencies extends beyond the concerns associated with more traditional settings.

Of Note:

- Criminal justice agencies are vulnerable to employee claims of sexual harassment by supervisors or coworkers, and may also be held responsible for the actions of nonemployees and for harassment directed at nonemployees.

- Acquiescence to requests for sexual favors--or even voluntary

* Paula N. Rubin, a lawyer, is a visiting fellow at the National Institute of Justice, coordinating NIJ's initiative to research, develop, and deliver publications and training for the criminal justice system on the Americans With Disabilities Act as well as other civil rights and human-resources management issues. This paper was prepared for the National Institute of Justice.

participation in sexual activity-- does not necessarily mean that the favors or activity were welcomed by a sexual harassment claimant.

➢ Workplace display of sexually explicit material- -photos, magazines, or posters--may constitute hostile work environment harassment, even though the private possession, reading, and consensual sharing of such materials is protected under the Constitution.

➢ While uncommon, a single severe incident of offending behavior may be sufficient to constitute hostile work environment harassment.

➢ An agency may investigate and take action where there is evidence of unwelcome conduct even if a complaint has not been filed.

➢ Failure to investigate promptly and take appropriate remedial action when a sexual harassment complaint has been filed may result in an agency being held liable for damages.

➢ Prevention--in the form of policy, training, supervision, and discipline--is the best way to avoid sexual harassment in the workplace.

Sexual harassment is not new, nor are legal remedies against it. It has been recognized for nearly 20 years as a form of sex discrimination under the Civil Rights Act of 1964. However, allegations of improper behavior in the business world and in all branches of government, at Federal, State, and local levels, have become commonplace in today's society. Inevitably, these have resulted in a heightened public awareness about sexual harassment. And, as the Nation's consciousness has risen so has the number of complaints alleging sexual harassment.

How is criminal justice affected by this issue? Obviously, allegations of sexual harassment in the workplace are not confined to the private sector. Police and corrections have their share of claims. Exposure to liability exists not only for the conduct of employees, but in the treatment of inmates, persons in custody or under supervision, and others having reason to interact with criminal justice professionals as well.

The intersection between sexual harassment and criminal justice can best be seen within a legal context. What is sexual harassment? How does this form of discrimination happen in the workplace? Finally, what can agencies do to limit their exposure to liability for claims of sexual harassment and to prevent it from happening within their ranks?

LEGAL OVERVIEW

The Civil Rights Act of 1964 (the Act) makes it illegal to discriminate on the basis of race, color, religion, age, national origin, and sex.[1] Title VII of the Act prohibits employers from, among other things, discriminating on the basis of sex with respect to compensation, terms, conditions, or privileges of employment. In addition, another form of sex discrimination is sexual harassment.

Sexual harassment in employment has been defined as unwelcome sexual advances, requests for sexual favors, and other verbal or physical conduct that enters into employment decisions and/or conduct that unreasonably interferes with an individual's work performance or creates an intimidating, hostile, or offensive working environment. This guideline identifies two forms of sexual harassment: (1) quid pro quo harassment; and (2) hostile work environment harassment. In the first type, the harasser demands sexual conduct as a condition for receiving a tangible benefit (note, however, a claimant might acquiesce to the demand, receive the benefit and nevertheless still have a claim).[2] In the second type, the work environment becomes so offensive as to adversely affect an employee's job performance.

Quid pro quo harassment. Loosely translated, "quid pro quo" means "something for something." This type of harassment occurs when an employee is required to choose between submitting to sexual advances or losing a tangible job benefit. An essential aspect of quid pro quo harassment is the harasser's power to control the employee's employment benefits. This kind of harassment most often occurs between supervisor and subordinate.

A claim of quid pro quo harassment must meet several criteria:

- The harassment was based on sex.

- The claimant was subjected to unwelcome sexual advances.

- A tangible economic benefit of the job was conditional on the claimant's submission to the unwelcome sexual advances.

In quid pro quo cases, the harassment consists of "unwelcome sexual advances, requests for sexual favors, and other verbal or physical conduct of a sexual nature."[3] However, there is no requirement that these requests be express demands for sexual favors.[4] The advances may be implied by the circumstances and actions: for example, inviting a claimant out for drinks or offering the claimant sexually explicit magazines.

A hallmark of a sexual harassment claim, whether it be quid pro quo or hostile work environment harassment, is that the advances are unwelcome. "Unwelcome" means that the person did not invite or solicit the advances. This is determined by an objective standard and not the claimant's subjective feelings.

On the other hand, acquiescence or even voluntary participation in sexual activity does not mean that the advances were not unwelcome.[5] One factor to consider is whether the person indicated that the advances were unwelcome notwithstanding acquiescence.

Hostile work environment harassment. Hostile work environment harassment is unwelcome conduct that is so severe or pervasive as to change the conditions of the claimant's employment and create an intimidating, hostile, or offensive work environment. In the landmark case of Meritor Savings Bank v. Vinson,[6] the U.S. Supreme Court found that a hostile work environment amounts to unlawful sex discrimination even in the absence of the loss of a tangible job benefit.

What distinguishes hostile work environment harassment from quid pro quo harassment? There are several differences. Hostile work environment harassment:

- Does not require an impact on an economic benefit.

- Can involve coworkers or third parties, not just supervisors.

- Is not limited to sexual advances; it can include hostile or offensive behavior based on the person's sex.

- Can occur even when the conduct is not directed specifically at the claimant but still impacts on his or her ability to perform the job.

- Typically involves a series of incidents rather than one incident (although a single offensive incident may constitute this type of harassment).

Three criteria must be met in a claim of harassment based on a hostile work environment:

- The conduct was unwelcome.

- The conduct was severe, pervasive, and regarded by the claimant as so hostile or offensive as to alter his or her conditions of employment.

- The conduct was such that a reasonable person would find it hostile or offensive.

Since this form of sexual harassment does not require the unwelcome conduct to involve sexual advances, other actions may give rise to a claim of hostile work environment. Obviously, gender-based actions such as calling the claimant derogatory names (including names referring to body parts or reproductive anatomy) could be actionable depending on the severity and the pervasiveness. Forms of hazing used to intimidate or dominate the claimant, such as insulting remarks, threats, or negative graffiti, may also constitute this type of harassment. Even actions not directed at a particular claimant may be considered hostile work environment harassment, e.g., the display of sexually explicit materials such as posters, pin-ups, and magazines.

In proving a claim of hostile work environment harassment, courts look at the totality of the circumstances. Severity and pervasiveness are pivotal. The more severe the conduct, the less pervasive it may need to be. Conversely, the more pervasive the conduct, the less severe it may need to be. That is why, although rare in hostile work environment cases, a single severe incident may still constitute this kind of harassment.[7] Severity of conduct may depend on whether the action is physically threatening or degrading, in contrast to offensive language. Pervasiveness is also more likely to be found in cases where there is more than one harasser.

A determining factor in a claim of hostile work environment harassment is that the conduct unreasonably interferes with the claimant's work performance.[8] "Unreasonable interference" means that the offensive conduct made it more difficult for the complainant to do his or her job.

By what standard is hostile work environment determined? Courts will generally use a "reasonable person" standard. That means that a reasonable person's work environment would be affected by the conduct. In addition, a 1991 circuit court decision allowed a female plaintiff to assert a "reasonable woman" standard.[9] This standard seeks to eliminate the perceptions that a reasonable male might have about what constitutes offensive, unwelcome conduct.

On the other hand, courts have refused to simply consider how the claimant perceived his or her work environment. In other words, Title VII does not serve as "a vehicle for vindicating the petty slights suffered by the hypersensitive."[10]

Must the claimant suffer injuries to prevail and, if so, how much? The U.S. Supreme Court offered guidance in the case of Harris v. Forklift.[11] To prevail on a claim of hostile work environment harassment, the conduct need not seriously affect an employee's psychological well-being nor cause an injury. The decisive issue is whether the conduct interfered with the claimant's work performance.

IMPLICATIONS FOR CRIMINAL JUSTICE

Sexual harassment may impact on criminal justice agencies in two ways. First, claims from employees expose the agency to liability in its capacity as an employer. Second, the agency may also be sued by third parties claiming to have been harassed by persons under the authority or control of the agency. Often these claims are brought under the Civil Rights Act of 1871 (42 U.S.C. Section 1983). Section 1983 imposes liability on any person who, under color of State law, deprives a person of rights guaranteed by Federal law.

Agency Liability

The degree to which a criminal justice agency can be held responsible for the actions of its employees depends on the type of harassment complaint filed and the identity of the claimant. Employers have consistently been found strictly liable for quid pro quo harassment by supervisors under their authority.

Strict liability is a legal standard that imposes liability even though the employer had no knowledge of the unlawful conduct. So, for example, if a superior officer makes sexual favors a condition of a subordinate's promotion, the department will be held liable even if it did not know about the superior officer's demands.

On the other hand, criminal justice agencies will not be automatically liable for claims by their employees of hostile work environment harassment. When hostile work environment harassment by a supervisor is alleged, employer liability will turn on such things as whether the employer had notice of the conduct, the means by which the harassment was committed, whether the claimant had the chance to complain about the conduct, what the employer did in response to any complaint or knowledge of the conduct, and what preventive and remedial measures the employer has taken. Some courts have, however, taken a broader approach to impose liability.[12]

When is the agency charged with knowledge of harassing conduct? That is, when will an agency without formal knowledge of the conduct be deemed to know that the offensive conduct exists? When a complaint is filed with someone high enough in the agency to infer notice to the agency; when supervisors see the offending conduct; or when the harassment is so pervasive that the agency should have known it was going on. For example, "pervasive graffiti and pornography can give rise to an inference of knowledge on the part of the employer."[13]

Agency liability is not limited to the abuse of power between supervisor and subordinate, nor the actions of co-workers. Inmates, suspects, arrestees, crime victims, and others having interaction with the agency can be involved in this unlawful conduct. In these instances the agency may be liable if the agency, its agents, or supervisory employees knew or should have known of the conduct but failed to take immediate action.

If a Complaint is Filed

An essential part of limiting an agency's liability for sexual harassment is the action it takes when a complaint is filed or, in cases where there is no complaint, when the agency knows or should have known of the offensive conduct. The worst thing an agency can do is nothing. A Federal jury in Los Angeles awarded $3.9 million to two female police officers who alleged that male co-workers sexually harassed them and their supervisors ignored their complaints.[14] Conversely, an employer's prompt and appropriate response to complaints can limit its liability.[15]

A failure to take prompt, remedial action can result in an agency being held liable for an award of damages. These may include back pay (limited to 2 years prior to the filing of an EEOC charge), front pay, and compensatory damages. Punitive damages, while recoverable by employees in the private sector, are not available to governmental employees.

Here are some steps to take when a complaint is filed:

- Act immediately. Take every complaint seriously. Do not assume that the problem will work itself out or go away on its own. A delay in taking action might be viewed as tacit approval of the conduct.

- Investigate and act on every complaint. This includes even those claims where victims minimize the incident(s). Often victims of sexual harassment are embarrassed or ashamed of the incident and may be reluctant to talk about it. The person responsible for handling sexual harassment complaints should conduct a thorough investigation or cause one to be conducted. Anyone and everyone involved in the incident(s) should be interviewed. Interviews should endeavor to answer who, what, where, how, and when. They should be conducted in private and their contents kept confidential.

- Keep accurate records of the investigation. It is a good idea to document all phases of the investigation from receipt of the complaint through any remedial action taken. These records may be valuable evidence of measures taken by the agency.

- Ensure that there is no retaliation against the complainant.

PREVENTING SEXUAL HARASSMENT

No matter how flawless the investigation or how quickly and fairly a complaint is handled by the agency, prevention is still the best approach to sexual harassment. Criminal justice agencies should consider building their prevention programs around four areas: policy, training, supervision, and discipline.

Policy

Every criminal justice agency should have a policy that clearly states that the agency prohibits any type of sexual harassment. However, having such a policy is not enough; it must be communicated to all employees and consistently and fairly enforced. To the extent practical, agencies should consider posting the policy for a period of time in employee work areas, locker rooms, or break rooms. Thereafter, copies should be kept in accessible locations. In addition, the policy should be included in any employee handbooks.

At a minimum, any sexual harassment policy should include:

- A statement that the criminal justice agency will not tolerate sexual harassment.
- A definition of sexual harassment, including examples of quid pro quo and hostile work environment harassment.
- A statement advising employees of the agency's grievance procedure and requiring employees to immediately report incidents.
- A statement that complaints will be taken seriously and investigated immediately.
- A statement of the penalty for violating the policy.
- A statement that all employees are to treat each other professionally and respectfully.

Training

Having a policy and talking about sexual harassment in a vacuum is often not enough. Criminal justice agencies should consider putting these ideas into a context to ensure that employees understand what sexual harassment is. Conducting sexual harassment training is an effective way to communicate the agency's policy.

Training should:

- Identify and describe forms of sexual harassment and give examples.
- Outline the agency's grievance procedure, explain how to use it, and discuss the importance of doing so.
- Discuss the penalty for violating the policy.
- Emphasize the need for a workplace free of harassment, offensive conduct, intimidation, or other forms of discrimination.

Supervision

A policy against sexual harassment is only as good as the supervisors who enforce it. For that reason, supervisors should be taught how to build and maintain a professional work environment.

Training should cover such matters as:

- How to spot sexual harassment.
- How to investigate complaints including proper documentation.
- What to do about observed sexual harassment, even when no complaint has been filed.
- How to keep the work environment as professional and nonhostile as possible.

Discipline

The agency's grievance procedure should be clearly delineated and communicated to all employees. In addition, to ensure that this grievance procedure is credible, it should be strictly and promptly followed. This is especially important since courts look at the action taken by employers in determining liability. When violations occur, proper disciplinary action should follow. Consider the following measures:

- Informing employees in advance of conduct that may result in immediate dismissal or in disciplinary action; in the latter case, describe the penalties involved.

- Following up on an incident, after an interval of time, to make sure the problem has not returned.

- Counseling all parties, and training (or retraining) all employees in cases where harassment has been alleged but cannot be determined.

- Repeating assurances that sexual harassment will not be tolerated.

CONCLUSION

Sexual harassment is as common to the field of criminal justice as to any other area of American enterprise, and the laws regarding how it should be regarded and dealt with apply to criminal justice agencies as much as to private sector workplaces. Awareness of the law and the consequences for disregarding it should guide criminal justice managers in effectively carrying out their responsibilities and avoiding liabilities for the agencies they administer.

NOTES

1 42 U.S.C. 2000-2(a)(1).
2 Kariban v. Columbia University, 14 F.3d 773 (2nd Cir. 1994).
3 EEOC Guideline 1604.11(a).
4 See: Nichols v. Frank 22, 9th Cir., December 12, 1994.
5 See: Kariban v. Columbia.
6 477 U.S. 57, 40 FEP Cases 1822 (1986).
7 Huitt v. Market Street Hotel Corp., 62 FEP 539 (D.Kan. 1993).
8 EEOC Guidelines 1604.11(a)(3).
9 Ellison v. Brady, 924 F.2d. 872, 54 FEP Cases 1346, republished as amended, 55 FEP Cases 111 (9th Cir. 1991); See also: Jensen v. Eveleth Taconite Co., 824 F. Supp. 847 (D. Minn. 1993).
10 Zabkowicz v. West Bend Co., 589 F. Supp. 780, 784, 35 EPD Par. 34, 766 (E.D. Wis. 1984).
11 114 S.Ct. 367 (1993).
12 See: Kariban v. Columbia.
13 Primer on Sexual Harassment, p. 59.
14 Clerkin v. City of Long Beach; Allison v. City of Long Beach, U.S. Dist. Ct. (CD Cal. 1991) as reported in Fire and Police Reporter, November 1991, p. 170.
15 Beardsley v. Isom, 828 F. Supp. 397 (E.D. Va. 1993); aff'd Beardsley v. Webb, 30 F.3d 524 (4th Cir. 1994).

HOMOSEXUALS AND U.S. MILITARY POLICY: CURRENT ISSUES

David F. Burrelli and Charles Dale

BACKGROUND AND ANALYSIS

Early in the 1992 presidential campaign, then-candidate Bill Clinton commented that, if elected, he would "lift the ban" on homosexuals serving in the military. The existing policy had been in place since the Carter Administration. The issue drew heated debate among policymakers and the public at large. In response to congressional concerns, President Clinton put into place an interim compromise that allowed the Department of Defense an opportunity to study the issues and develop a "draft executive order" that would end discrimination on the basis of "sexual orientation." This interim compromise (announced on January 29, 1993) also provided Congress additional time to more fully exercise its constitutional authority under Article I, Section 8, clause 14, "To make rules for the Government and Regulation of the land and naval forces," including the consideration of legislation and the holding of hearings on the issue. One of the elements of the compromise was an agreement within the Congress not to immediately consider legislation that would have enacted into law the existing regulations.[1]

The Senate Armed Services (SASC) held extensive hearings on the issue. The House Armed Services Committee (HASC) has also held hearings. By

[1] See Congressional Record, February 4, 1993, S1263-S1339.

May 1993, a congressional consensus appeared to emerge over what then-SASC chairman Sam Nunn described as a "don't ask, don't tell" approach. Under this approach, the Department of Defense would not ask questions concerning the homosexuality of prospective members of the military, and individuals would be required to keep their homosexuality to themselves or be discharged if already in the service or denied enlistment/appointment if seeking to join the service.

On July 19, 1993, President Clinton announced his compromise: "don't ask, don't tell, don't pursue." The inclusion of "don't pursue" (akin to a "don't investigate" stance advocated by homosexual rights group) seemingly created a contradiction in the President's policy. On the one hand, it maintains the notion of military necessity and privacy as found in the congressional compromise of "don't ask, don't tell," and then appears to prevent efforts to enforce regulations and laws by limiting the military necessity and privacy as found in the congressional compromise of "don't ask, don't tell," and then appears to prevent efforts to enforce regulations and laws by limiting the military's role via "don't pursue." This problem was discussed at hearings with then-Secretary of Defense Les Aspin. Secretary Aspin indicated at one moment that individuals could acknowledge their homosexuality without risking an investigation or discharge; later he said that individual statements may not be credible grounds for investigating if the commander so decided but, if investigated, such statements could be credible grounds for a discharge proceeding. Ultimately, the Secretary agreed that statements are grounds for investigations and discharge.

The President's policy is based on sexual "orientation." This term has generated problems concerning its practical definition. This policy also declared:

> A Service member may also be separated if he or she states that he or she is a homosexual or bisexual, or words to that effect. Such a statement creates a rebuttable presumption that the member engages in homosexual acts or has a propensity or intent to do so. The Service member will have the opportunity to rebut that presumption however, by

> demonstrating that he or she does not engage in homosexual acts and does not have a propensity or intent to do so.[2]

In hearings, Senators raised numerous questions as to what behavior, if any, would justify the commencement of an investigation, and what grounds would justify the commencement of an investigation, and what grounds would justify an administrative discharge. Since commanders and noncommissioned officers are not usually lawyers, many critics argued that such rules created legal technicalities that would prove dysfunctional in a military setting and/or lead to an expansion of unpredictable court remedies. Some have argued that this outcome would not displease the Administration even if it was not the original intent. The thesis here is that this implementation of the compromise policy would encourage judicial intervention and, thereby, would provide a means to seek a judicial resolution asserting the compromise is unconstitutional. These critics note that the task of defending the compromise is left in control of the Administration via the Justice Department and hypothesize that the Administration could implement a muddled regulation, await a legal challenge, then poorly defend the policy, thereby encouraging judicial intervention in finding the policy unconstitutional. Other observers have noted that the President was merely trying to pursue a compromise that would take into account the concerns of the Congress and the military, but would also minimize discrimination against homosexuals.

On November 30, 1993, the FY1994 National Defense Authorization Act was signed into law by President Clinton (P.L. 103-160). In many ways, this law was a reiteration of the pre-1993 policy. Viewing homosexuality in the ranks as an "unacceptable risk...to morale, good order, and discipline," the law codifies the grounds for discharge: 1) the member has engaged in, attempted to engage in or solicited another to engage in a homosexual act or acts; 2) the member states that he or she is a homosexual or bisexual; or 3) the member has married or attempted to marry someone of the same sex. The law also states that DOD will brief new entrants (accessions) and members on a regular basis. Finally, the law instructs that asking questions of new recruits concerning sexuality may be resumed - having been halted in January, 1993 – on a discretionary don't ask, definitely don't tell" policy.

---

[2] Office of the Assistant Secretary of Defense, (Public Affairs), News Release, December 22, 1993.

On December 22, 1993, Secretary of Defense Aspin released new DOD regulations to implement the statute enacted the preceding month. Language in these regulations indicated that the Secretary was trying to incorporate both the restrictions in the law, and the President's desire to open military service "to those who have a homosexual orientation." (For example, the policy stated that "sexual orientation is considered a personal and private matter, and homosexual orientation is not a bar to service entry or continued service unless manifested by homosexual conduct." According to this statement of DOD regulations "Sexual orientation" was defined as "A sexual attraction to individuals of a particular sex.") However, with Aspin's resignation and the confirmation of William Perry as the new Secretary of Defense in February 1994, DOD reportedly accepted the recommendation of certain Senators to delete from DOD regulations the phrase, "homosexual orientation…is not a bar to military service."[3] In its place, DOD inserted the statement:

> A person's sexual orientation is considered a personal and private matter, and is not a bar to service unless manifested by homosexual content.[4]

In addition, the definition of "sexual orientation" was also modified:

> An abstract sexual preference for persons of a particular sex, as distinct from a propensity or intent to engage in sexual acts.

The elusiveness of the definition of "orientation" is apparent. Under the Administration's original definition, "orientation" is a sexual attraction. Under the revised definition, it is "personal and private," DOD is not to ask and personnel are not to tell. Should an individual choose to make his or her homosexual "orientation" public – i.e., no longer private and personal, nor abstract – an investigation and discharge are likely to result.

The ambiguous nature of the term "orientation" and its usage has not been without problems. In 1994, a Navy tribunal decided not to discharge Lt. Maria Z. Dunning after she had made the statement "I am a lesbian" at a January 1993 rally. Her attorneys argued that she was not broadcasting her intentions

---

[3] Scarborough, Rowan, White House Cuts Phrase Restricting Gay Discharges, *Washington Times*, February, 10, 1994.

[4] See Defense Policy on Gays Takes Effect, *Washington Post*, March 2, 1994.

to practice homosexuality but merely acknowledging her "sexual orientation." In the view of the reviewing officers, she had successfully rebutted the presumption that she would commit homosexual acts. Such finding, if not at least inconsistent with the intent of law and regulations, created a legal avenue via which homosexuals could announce their sexuality without being discharged. Shortly afterward, the Department of Defense Office of the General Counsel released a memo, in August 1995, addressing this issue:

> A member may not avoid the burden of rebutting the presumption merely by asserting that his or her statement of homosexuality was intended to convey only a message about sexual orientation..., and not to convey any message about propensity or intent to engage in homosexual acts. To the contrary, by virtue of the statement, the member bears the burden of proof that he or she does not engage in, and does not attempt, have a propensity, [n] or intend to engage in homosexual acts. IF the member in rebuttal offers evidence that he or she does not engage in homosexual acts or have a propensity or intent to do so, the offering of the evidence does not shift the burden of proof to the government. Rather, the burden of proof remains on the member throughout the proceeding.

DISCHARGE STATISTICS

Recent reports in the media have stated that since the implementation of the "don't ask, don't tell" policy, the number of discharges for homosexuality have increased. Homosexual rights advocates cite these data as evidence that the military "has resumed witch hunts."

According to the General Accounting Office (GAO):

> During the fiscal years 1980 through 1990, approximately 17,000 servicemen and women (an average of about 1,500 per

year) were separated from the services under the category of "homosexuality."[5]

GAO noted that the number of discharges peaked in 1982 and declined thereafter. The data on the number of DOD discharges is presented below. Data for the years 1980 through 1990 are from GAO. Data from 1991 through 1998 are from DOD. On average. 0.063 percent of total active duty discharges are for homosexual conduct. Homosexual advocacy groups claim that such an increase in discharges represents anti-homosexual harassment or witch hunts.[6] Conversely, it has been noted that certain individuals are using the "don't tell" provisions as a simple means of voiding their contractual commitment and hanging the bill for training and other expenses on the taxpayer.[7] Nevertheless, charges of "witch hunts" are difficult to support considering the relatively small percentage (0.063 percent) of such discharges given estimated prevalence of homosexuality in the general population is 1.6 percent.[8]

In April 1998, the Department of Defense, released its review of the implementation of this policy. This review was allegedly instituted after complaints were aired that the increasing rate of discharges were a sign of "witch hunts." In its review, DOD concluded that "for the most part, the policy has been properly applied and enforced."

---

[5] U.S. General Accounting Office, Defense Force Management: DOD's Policy on Homosexuality, B-247235, June 12, 1992; see also, U.S. General Accounting Office, Defense Force Management: Statistics Related to DOD's Policy on Homosexuality, B-247234, June 12, 1992.

[6] Myers, Steven Lee, Gay Group's Study Finds Military Harassment Rising, *The New York Times,* March 15, 1999.

[7] The Air Force released a statement claiming "...in 'virtually' all cases trainees volunteered that they were gay, probably to escape military service," Parker, Richard, Air Force Base in Texas 'Weeding Out' Gays?, *Knight Ridder Newspapers,* January 26, 1999.

[8] Smith, Tom W., Adult Sexual Behavior in 1989: Number of Partners, Frequency of Intercourse and Risk of AIDS, Family Planning Perspectives, Vol. 23, No. 3, May/June 1991: 104. We are unaware of any reliable empirical research supporting the near mythical claim that homosexuals account for 10% of the population. However, if such a claim were true, the notion that the military was conducting witch hunts by discharging only 0.063% would be even more difficult to sustain.

Table 1
Homosexual Conduct Administrative Separation Discharge Statistics

Fiscal Year	Total Number of Homosexual Discharges	Percentage of Total Active Force
1980	1,75	0.086
1981	1,817	0.088
1982	1,998	0.095
1983	1,815	0.086
1984	1,822	0.086
1985	1,660	0.078
1986	1,664	0.076
1987	1,380	0.064
1988	1,100	0.052
1989	997	0.047
1990	932	0.046
1991	949	0.047
1992	708	0.039
1993	682	0.039
1994	597	0.037
1995	610**	0.039
1996	850	0.039
1997	997	0.069
1998	1,145	0.081

** According to DOD: "The total figure is normalized to compensate for 163 Air Force discharges that under the old policy have been characterized as "fraudulent enlistment" and are now characterized as 'for homosexual conduct.' Under the old policy, recruits who answered 'no' when asked if they were homosexual on enlistment. Under the new policy, that question is no longer asked in the enlistment." In addition, claims of harassment at training depots have not been supported by interviews with recruits.[9]

[9] Christenson, Sig, Recruits Deny Lackland Harassment, *San Antonio Express-News,* February 7, 1999. This and other articles show that claims of homosexuality can serve as a means of terminating a military obligation. "Mario isn't in the Army now. In March he left Fort Bragg with an honorable discharge. Some may find Mario's willingness to use his homosexuality as a

ISSUES

Legal Challenges

Constitutional challenges to former and contemporary military policies regarding homosexuals began to accelerate following enactment of the "don't ask, don't tell" compromise between Congress and the President. A lengthy tradition of "special deference" to the military led most federal district and appeals courts to affirm the "considered professional judgment" of military leaders to discipline or discharge a service member for homosexual conduct or speech. Based on the U.S. Supreme Court ruling in *Bowers v. Hardwick*[10] that there is no fundamental right to engage in consensual homosexual sodomy, the courts ruled that the military could constitutionally discharge a service member for overt homosexual behavior. Judicial challenges to "don't ask, don't tell" focused on the "statements" provision of the new policy which presumes, absent contrary evidence, homosexual activity or a "propensity" to act on the part of any service member who acknowledges his/her homosexuality. The High Court has refused to review the military's "don't ask, don't tell" policy on five separate occasions, most recently on January 19, 1999, when it denied the appeal of two former service members who were discharged after declaring their homosexuality to commanding officers. Without comment, the Justices turned aside arguments that the policy was based on prejudice against homosexuals and violates their free speech rights.[11] The impact of the Supreme Court ruling in *Romer v. Evans*[12] on the legal developments in this area has been minimal. As discussed below, the courts in the military discharge cases already apply a rationality standard of equal protection similar to that invoked by the *Romer* Court to defeat Colorado's "Amendment 2," and far greater judicial tolerance generally has marked scrutiny into affairs of the military than civilian authorities.

Three federal district courts in the Ninth Circuit ruled that the pre-1993 military policy violated the Constitution's Equal Protection guarantee since it was not rationally related to the government's declared objective of

means of shirking his commitment objectionable." Lamme, Robert, Dazed in the Military, *The Advocate*, No. 673, January 24, 1995: 46

[10] 478 U.S. 186 (1986).

[11] Holmes v. California Army National Guard, No. 98-500, 119 S. Ct. 794 (1999).

[12] 517 U.S. 620 (1969).

"discipline, good order, and morale." In *Meinhold v. United States,*[13] the district court found in favor of a service member who had disclosed his homosexual "orientation" on a national television news program and enjoined the Department of Defense from "discharging or denying enlistment to any person based on sexual orientation in the absence of sexual conduct which interferes with the military mission..." On appeal, the Ninth Circuit recognized that equating status with prohibited acts or conduct is "problematic," but avoided reaching the constitutional question because it construed the former policy as permitting discharge from service only where the service member makes "statements that show a concrete, fixed, or express desire to commit homosexual acts." Meinhold's "statement of orientation alone and...his classification as a homosexual," arbitrarily went beyond what DOD's policy seeks to prevent." Similarly, in *Cammermeyer v. Aspin*[14] and *Dahl v. Secretary of Navy,*[15] the old exclusion policy was found unconstitutional by federal district courts applying the traditional "rational basis" standard of equal protection review.

Those courts upholding the old policy equated homosexual "orientation" with homosexual conduct as a potential threat to unit cohesion and combat readiness and decided that the "military need not wait until a homosexual acts on his or her sexual desires."[16]. *Steffan v. Perry*[17]reviewed the separation of an admitted homosexual midshipman whose request for a diploma from the U.S. Naval Academy was denied after he was forced to resign shortly before graduation. Because "the class of self-described homosexuals is significantly close to the class of those who engage or intend to engage in homosexual conduct," and "homosexuality, like all forms of sexual orientation, is tied closely to sexual conduct" the en banc majority concluded that both the Naval Academy mandatory discharge regulation and 1982 DOD Directive were constitutional. In addition, the "special deference we owe the military's judgment" influenced the scope of the court's inquiry into the "rationality of the military's policy." Steffan decided not to appeal the D.C. Circuit's

---

[13] 808 F. Supp. 1455 (C.D. Cal. 1993), *aff'd in part and rev'd and vacated in part*, 34 F. 3d 1469 (9th Cir. 1994).

[14] 850 F. Supp. 910 (W.D. Wash. 1994), *dismissed as moot* 97 F. 3d 1235 (9th Cir. 1996).

[15] 830 F. Supp. 1319 (E.D. Cal. 1993).

[16] *Ben-Shalom v. Marsh* 881 F. 2d 454, 464 (7th Cir. 1989).

[17] 41 F.3d 677 (D.C. Cir. 1994).

decision, creating some tension between the D. C. Circuit and the Ninth Circuit in *Meinhold* concerning the pre-1993 policy.

The Fourth Circuit was the first federal appeals court to uphold the military's "don't ask, don't tell" policy towards homosexuals. The plaintiff, Lt. Paul G. Thomasson, was honorably discharged under the policy after he announced in March 1994 that he was homosexual. Writing for the nine-member majority in *Thomasson v. Perry,*[18] Chief Judge J. Harvie Wilkinson III stressed Congress' "plenary control" of the military and the "deference" owed both the Executive and Legislative Branches in matters of national defense as factors calling for judicial restraint when faced with challenges to military decision making. "What Thomasson challenges," the opinion notes, "is the statute that embodies the exhaustive efforts of the democratically accountable branches of American government and an enactment that reflects month upon month of political negotiation and deliberation." Consequently, because "homosexuals do not constitute a suspect class," the court declined to apply "strict scrutiny" to the plaintiff's equal protection claims and settled for "rational basis review" as the proper constitutional standard.

Upon this standard Judge Wilkinson concluded that the government articulated a "legitimate purpose" for excluding individuals who commit homosexual acts - that of maintaining unit cohesion and military readiness – and that the law's rebuttable presumption was a "rational means" of preventing individuals who engage in, or have presumption was a "rational means" of preventing individuals who engage ink or have a "propensity' to engage in, homosexual conduct from serving in the military. "Given that it is legitimate for Congress to proscribe homosexual acts, it is also legitimate for the government to seek to forestall these same dangers by trying to prevent the commission of such acts." Similarly, Thomasson's First Amendment claims were rejected for the reason that "[t]he statute does not target speech declaring homosexuality; rather it targets homosexual acts and the propensity or intent to engage in homosexual acts, and permissibly uses the speech as evidence. The use of speech as evidence in this manner does not raise a constitutional issue - the First Amendment does not prohibit the evidentiary use of speech to establish the elements of a crime, or, as is the case here, to prove motive or intent." In a *per curiam* ruling, the Fourth Circuit relied on Thomasson to affirm a ruling by federal district judge Ellis in *Thorne v. U. S. Department of*

---

[18] 80 F.3d 915 (4th Cir.), *cert. Denied,* 117 S. Ct. 356 (1996).

Defense.[19] After reviewing the record in eight other administrative separation proceedings where the presumption that a declared homosexual has a propensity to engage in forbidden conduct was successfully rebutted, Judge Ellis concluded in *Thorne* that conduct rather than speech was the target of the "don't ask, don't tell" policy.[20]

In *Richenberg v. Perry*, 97 F. 3d 256 (8th Cir. 1996) *cert. denied,* 118 S. Ct. 45 (1997), the Eighth Circuit upheld the statements provision of "don't ask, don't tell" as applied to the discharge of an Air Force captain who had informed his commanding officer that he was homosexual. As in *Thomasson*, the policy was alleged to violate equal protection and free speech rights by targeting declarations of "homosexual orientation or status" unrelated to conduct and for "irrational catering to prejudice against and hatred of homosexuals." Agreeing with the Fourth Circuit, however, the *Richenberg* court found that the policy ban on homosexual acts was justified by legitimate military needs and rationally served by the rebuttable presumption of a "propensity" to act on the part of declared homosexuals. It pointed to instances of seven service members who had successfully rebutted the presumption as an indication that the policy was not being applied to penalize homosexual status alone. Similarly, because the focus of "don't ask, don't tell" is to "identify and exclude those who are likely to engage in homosexual acts," while prohibiting direct inquiries into an applicant's sexual orientation, there was no basis for a First Amendment challenge, the court concluded.

In appeals from three district court rulings during 1997, the Ninth Circuit approved the discharge of a naval petty officer who admitted to sexual relations with other men, *Philips v. Perry*,[21] and of a California National Guardsman and Navy lieutenant who had submitted written documents to their commanding officers acknowledging that they were homosexual.[22] In the former case, the appeals court ruled that homosexuals are not members of a "suspect class" for purposes of federal equal protection analysis, that the military ban on homosexual "acts" was rationally related to legitimate

[19] 945 F. Supp. 924 (E.D> Va. 1996), aff'd per curiam, 139 F.3d 893 (4th Cir. 1998)

[20] See also Selland v. Perry, 905 F. Supp. 260 (E. D. Md 1995), where the district court decided that the Navy could constitutionally separate a service member for prohibited homosexual acts based on inferences drawn from his statement that he was homosexual and in a monogamous relationship.

[21] 106 F.3d 1420 (9the Cir. 1997).

governmental interest in "maintaining effective armed forces," and that evidentiary use of admitted homosexuality did not violate a service member's First Amendment rights. Because sufficient homosexual acts were alleged to justify discharge, the *Perry* court declined considering the constitutionality of the rebuttable presumption and statements prong of the military policy. That issue was revisited in presumption and statements prong of the military policy. That issues was revisited in *Holmes* and *Watson*, however, where the Ninth Circuit ruled that military personnel who "tell," without also presenting evidence to rebut the inference that they engage in homosexual acts, may constitutionally be discharged from the service. Writing for a divided three-judge panel, Circuit Judge Wiggins "agreed[d] with the Second, Fourth, and Eighth Circuits on this issue. Although the legislature's assumption that declared homosexuals will engage in homosexuals will engage in homosexual conduct is imperfect, it is sufficiently rational to survive [equal protection] scrutiny…"[23]

The new law regarding homosexuals in the military has been before the Second Circuit on two rounds of appeals from rulings by District Judge Eugene Nickerson. Initially, Judge Nickerson disapproved of the "statements presumption" in the laws as an impermissible "content" restriction on free speech rights, finding that it penalized "a mere statement of homosexual orientation" with only a "hypothetical" opportunity for rebuttal. However, discerning a "strong correlation" between homosexual statements and likely conduct, the appeals court noted approval of the presumption at a preliminary stage.[24] Nonetheless, because the speech and conduct provisions of the law had to "rise and fall together," the Second Circuit remanded the case for further consideration of the equal protection issue surrounding the military prohibition on homosexual acts. Judge Nickerson then became the first federal judge to strike down both the "acts" and "statements" provision of the policy. In answering the question posed by the Second Circuit, the district court concluded that the conduct portion of the policy, like the speech portion, was

---

[22] *Holmes v. California Army National Guard; Watson v. Cohen,* 124 F.3d 1126 (9th Cir 1997), cert. Denied, No. 98-500, 119 S. Ct. 794 (1999).

[23] 124 F. 3d at 1135. See also Jackson v. Department of the Air Force, 132 F. 3d 39 (9th Cir. 1997) (holding that homosexuals are not members of a suspect class, that the military's regulations are rationally related to a legitimate government interest, and are not arbitrary or irrational.

[24] *Able v. United States*, 88 F. 3d 1280 (2nd Dir. 1996).

impermissibly premised upon "animosity of heterosexuals" and lacked a rational basis. "Unit cohesion" was seen as a "euphemism for catering to the prejudices of heterosexuals" and was an illegitimate reasons for government sanctioned discrimination against gay and lesbian service members.

On September 23, 1998, the federal appeals court issued its latest ruling in *Able v. Untied States.*[25] Aligning itself with the collective opinion from other circuits, the appeals court faulted Judge Nickerson for failing to give proper deference to Congress and the military judgment and upheld the "don't ask, don't tell" policy. The opinion emphasizes a judicial tradition of applying "less stringent standards" of constitutional review to military rules than to laws and regulations governing civilian society. Judicial deference was warranted by the need for discipline and unit cohesion within this "specialized community," matters for which courts "are ill-suited to second-guess military judgments that bear upon military capability and readiness." In addition, "extensive Congressional hearings and deliberation" provided a "rational basis" for the government's contention that the prohibition on homosexual conduct "promotes unit cohesion, enhances privacy and reduces sexual tension." Consequently, the court concluded, "[g]iven the strong presumption of validity we give to classifications under rational basis review and the special respect accorded to Congress' decisions regarding military matters, we will not substitute our judgment for that of Congress."

McVeigh v. Cohen[26] enjoined the discharge of a sailor under the new policy due to allegations of the Navy's failure to follow its own rules rather than on constitutional grounds. The naval investigation of McVeigh, a 17-year veteran sailor serving on a nuclear-powered submarine based in Honolulu, was prompted by an e-mail message sent by him under the alias "Boyrsch" to a civilian Navy employee who was organizing a toy drive for the children of Navy crew members. A search of the "member profile directory" of American Online revealed that the sender of the message was a member of the military in Honolulu named "Tim" who identified his marital status as "gay." This information was eventually forwarded to a naval investigator who, without identifying himself, contacted America Online and received confirmation that the sender of the message in question was McVeigh. After an administrative hearing, McVeigh was discharged on the basis of homosexuality.

[25] 155 F. 3d 628 (2d Cir. 1998).

[26] 996 F. Supp 59 (D. D. C. 1998).

A temporary injunction blocking the sailor's discharge was subsequently made permanent by U. S. District Judge Stanley Sporkin. He found that the Navy had arguably violated its own rules against investigating gay service members without "credible information" of homosexual acts or statements. In the "virtual reality" of cyberspace, said the court, "suggestions of sexual orientation in a private, anonymous email account"—while possibly supporting a "belief" or "suspicion" of homosexual conduct—did not amount to a declaration of homosexuality warranting an investigation. "Even if the Navy had a factual basis to believe that he email message and profile were written by plaintiff, it was unreasonable to infer that they were necessarily intended to convey a propensity or intent to engage in homosexual conduct." In addition, Judge Sporkin suggested but did not rule on whether or not the naval investigators had violated the Electronic Communications Privacy Act of 1986. That law requires that before a government agency may obtain personal information from a computer service provider, it must have a subpoena, court order or the subject's consent, none of which the Navy had. Although this decision has been claimed as a "victory for gay rights," some have argued that Judge Sporkin made a calculated judgment that this Administration would not appeal his decision. An appeal was sought by the Navy but opposed by the Justice Department and White House. McVeigh settled with the Navy. Under the settlement, McVeigh would retire from the Navy and receive a payment for legal fees.

ROTC and Campus Policies

Many college and university (and in some cases, high school) campuses have been in the vanguard of the effort to expand civil rights for homosexuals. In certain cases, schools have sought to challenge DOD policy pertaining to homosexuals including taking steps to limit or eliminate the military presence on campus. Military personnel have been prevented from recruiting on campus, and action has been taken to limit or sever Reserve Officer Training Corps (ROTC) connections with the campus. Rather than attacking ROTC, some schools (sometimes with state support) have taken a broader approach of preventing recruiters from having access to the campus because of objections to DOD's policies concerning homosexuals.

Even prior to the 1993 compromise, the exclusion of homosexuals from ROTC had proven to be problematic. (From 1986 to 1994, 28 students were discharged from ROTC on grounds of homosexuality and nine were ordered to repay their scholarships.) In May 1990, two students from Harvard and the Massachusetts Institute of Technology were dismissed from the Navy ROTC program at MIT. The Navy sought recoupment of its scholarship funds (totaling over $80,000 for both students). The provost of MIT, John Deutch, wrote to then-Secretary of Defense Richard Cheney, stating that it was "wrong and shortsighted" to maintain "The ROTC policy not to accept gay or lesbian students into its programs and to require avowed homosexuals to disenroll and pay back their scholarship funds."[27] After reviewing the cases, the Navy terminated its efforts to seek recoupment from these two students.

On May 17, 1994, then-Deputy Defense Secretary John Deutch issued a directive. Under that directive, and based on the "don't ask, don't tell compromise, service secretaries can seek recoupment of ROTC scholarships when there are violations of military law. However, secretaries are no longer forced to seek recoupment. In some respects, the recoupment policy seeks to draw a distinction between behavior and "orientation." According to the *Air Force Times*, "acts short of sodomy" do not constitute a basis for recoupment, but if the student is discharged for criminal conduct or under less than honorable conditions, recoupment procedures could be expected with the final decision resting with the secretary concerned. Likewise, individuals using a claim of homosexuality as a means of avoiding military service are likely to be required to repay their scholarships.[28] John Deutch was later selected by President Clinton to be the Director of Central Intelligence.

In response to these issues, legislation was enacted in the National Defense Authorization Act for FY1995[29] to limit efforts to interfere with military access to schools.

> No funds available to the Department of Defense may be provided by grant or contract to any institution of higher education that has a policy of denying, or which effectively prevents, the Secretary of Defense from obtaining for military

[27] Lewin, Tamar, Navy Drops Efforts to seek Repayment From 2 Gay Students, *New York Times*, May 9, 1990: 19.).

[28] See Hudson, Neff, Gays ousted from ROTC get break, *Air Force Times*, June 27, 1994.

[29] P. L. 103-337, October 5, 1994, 108 Stat. 2776.

> recruiting purposes – (A) entry to campuses or access to students on campuses; or (B) access to directory information pertaining to students.

The law further instructs the Secretary of Defense to consult with the Secretary of Education in prescribing regulations to determine when an educational institution denies or prevents access.

More recently, Congress enacted language pertaining to ROTC. The National Defense Authorization Act for FY1996[30] states:

> No funds appropriated or otherwise available to the Department of Defense may be made obligated by contract or by grant (including a grant of funds to be available for student aid) to any institution of higher education that, as determined by the Secretary of Defense, has an anti-ROTC policy and at which, as determined by the Secretary, the Secretary would otherwise maintain or seek to establish a unit of the Senior Reserve Officer Training Corps or at which the Secretary would otherwise enroll or seek to enroll students for participation in a unit of the Senior Reserve Officer Training Corps at another nearby institution of higher education.

This law requires the Secretary to notify the Secretary of Education, Senate Armed Services Committee and the then-House National Security Committee (now House Armed Services Committee) when such a determination has been made. In addition, every 6 months the Secretary is required to publish a list of ineligible institutions in the Federal Register.

Recently, the Connecticut Supreme Court upheld a lower court ruling that the DOD policy on homosexuality violates the state's "gay rights law" barring discrimination on the basis of sexual "orientation" and, therefore, military recruiters could be permanently banned from the Law School campus in Hartford.[31]

---

[30] P. L. 104-106, February 10, 1996, Section 541.

[31] *Gay and Lesbian Law Students Association v. Board of Trustees*, 236 Conn. 453, 673 A.2d 484 (Conn. 1996.).

These actions in Connecticut have led to a baffling situation. The University of Connecticut (UConn) has been designated, by the state legislature, a land-grant university. Under the Morrill Act, as signed by President Lincoln in 1862,institutions aided under the act must teach military tactics along with their regular curriculum. Generally speaking, ROTC has served to fulfill this requirement. (During the 1995-96 school year, a total of over 160 students participated in ROTC at UConn. The Air Force and Army have ROTC programs at UConn. UConn also sponsors those partaking in ROTC from Yale University since no such program is available at the Yale campus.) Thus, military recruiters were prohibited from recruiting at the university's law school in Hartford, but the university maintains an ROTC unit at its campus in Storrs. This campus continued to enroll students in ROTC and accepted federal funding. The presence of, and continued enrollment by, this ROTC unit would arguably conflict with the state's gay rights law.

Finally, a faculty task force at the Massachusetts Institute of Technology has recommended that MIT open its ROTC unit to avowed homosexuals, in direct conflict with federal law. MIT's ROTC unit also hosts students from Harvard, Tufts, and Wellesley.) Under the new law, MIT could reportedly lose $56 million in annual defense contracts. Officials at both MIT and DOD have stated that they are working on resolving this apparent conflict.[32]

The Omnibus Appropriations for FY1997[33] contained language that limits the ability of educational institutions , or sub-elements thereof (such as a law schools or a satellite campus), to block ROTC programs or recruiter access. Under this language, no funds made available in this or other relevant appropriations, including contracts or grants (such as student aid), are available to any covered institution that denies or prevents access by military recruiters or prevents the maintaining, establishing or the operation of an ROTC program. Three exceptions were written into the law: (1) :"the covered educational entity has ceased the policy or practice [of discriminating against the military]; (2) the institution of higher education has a longstanding policy of pacifism based on historical religious affiliation; or (3) the institution of higher education involved is prohibited by the law of any State, or by the order of any State court, from allowing Senior Reserve Officer Training Corps

[32] See Scarborough, Rowan, MIT may quit ROTC over homosexuality, *Washington Times*, April 3, 1996: A4.

[33] P. L. 104-208, September 30, 1996.

activities or Federal recruiting on campus, except that this paragraph shall apply only during the one-year period beginning of the effective date…" In the summer of 1997, DOD published a list of offending schools. Of the 27 schools on the list, 17 were in Connecticut. By August 22, 1997, the list was reduced to 22 schools, 17 from Connecticut.

In a seemingly ironic twist, service members who receive tuition assistance from the military would see this assistance terminated if they attended one of the school listed. Clearly, this was not the intent of the language's sponsors. In order to address this situation, language was included in the 1998 DOD Authorization Act conference report:

> The conferees are aware that the Connecticut State Legislature and the State Supreme Court have taken steps to prohibit military recruiting on the campuses of state funded colleges and universities. As a result of this prohibition, …the Department of Defense suspended payment of contract and grant funding to these college and universities.
>
> The conferees note that the Connecticut State Legislature is not scheduled to meet until February 1998. The Governor has pledged that he will ensure the passage of legislation that would remedy the matter concerning access of military recruiters to Connecticut state institutions of higher education.
>
> In order to provide the State of Connecticut with the opportunity to repeal its prohibition, the conferees direct the Secretary of Defense not to use funds that would have been used for contracts or grants to higher education institutions in Connecticut as sources in a reprogramming request nor to submit such funds as part of a recession offer until March 29, 1998. If the State of Connecticut has not repealed the prohibition as of March 29, 1998, the Secretary of Defense may use the funds in a reprogramming or recession activity.
>
> Notwithstanding this sequestering of funds, the conferees insist that military recruiters be afforded access to institutions of higher education or face the consequence of loss of federal funds.[34]

[34] Congressional Record, Oct 23, 1997: H9383.

As of Oct. 9, 1997, in addition to the 17 schools in Connecticut, only two other Schools were reported to be at risk of losing federal funding: the Washington College of Law at American University in Washington, D. C., and the William Mitchell College of Law in St. Paul, MN.

Since publishing the first list in July, the number of schools on the list has dropped virtually every month s they have dropped their anti-recruiting, anti-ROTC policies. The biggest decrease came in November, when Connecticut changed its state law and its 17 colleges fell off the list. Now comes the latest list, published in the Jan. 28 Federal Register. Number of schools on the list: zero.[35]

More recently, two high schools broke with the Portland School Board by allowing military recruiters on campus, thereby ending the only known recruiting ban on recruiters in a public school system.[36] Proponents of the ban insist they are opposing discrimination against homosexuals by the military. Critics contend the school board is merely, and hypocritically, substituting, discrimination against the military in favor of a "homosexual rights agenda."

HOMOSEXUALS AND MARRIAGES

Under current law, marriages are covered under the domestic relations laws of the various states. A legal ruling by Hawaii's Circuit Court (on remand by the State Supreme Court) held that the state may not prohibit same-sex marriages.

Under a different law, as well as the pre-1993 regulations, the Department of Defense does not define marriage, per se. Instead the department relies on state definitions of marriage in providing benefits to married members of the armed services and their dependents. However, current law denies enlistment or continued service to anyone who "has married or attempted to marry someone of the same sex." In other words, even if a state recognized a same sex marriage, federal law requires that any member of such a union would be denied enlistment or continued service in the armed services, i. e., be discharged. Since Hawaii would recognize same-sex marriages, it is unclear what, if any, federal benefits would accrue to a same-sex spouse via DOD (or

[35] Navy Times, Feb. 9, 1998: 28.

[36] Two schools defy district ban on military recruiters, Associated Press, December 24, 1998.

the Dept, of Veterans Affairs) based on military service, regardless of when the marriage occurs. For example, it is possible for a member to serve 20 years and retire from the military. The retiree could then marry in a state that recognizes same-sex marriages and seek to provide survivor benefits to the spouse under the military Survivor Benefit Plan. Without a Federal definition of "marriage," efforts to deny benefits to same-sex spouses, or treat them differently from heterosexual marriages, are likely to face court challenges.

Federal legislation has been enacted that would limit reciprocal interstate recognition of same-sex marriages. This legislation also defines "marriage" for Federal agencies as the "legal union between one man and one woman as husband and wife, [with] the word 'spouse' refer[ring] only to a person of the opposite sex who is a husband or a wife."[37] H. R. 3396 was passed by the house on July 12, 1996 by a 342-67 vote. On September 10, 1996, the Senate passed the Defense of Marriage Act. The President signed the bill into law on September 21, 1996.[38]

SECURITY CLEARANCES

On August 2, 1995, President Clinton signed Executive Order 12968 (Access to Classified Information). Part of this Executive Order removed "sexual orientation" as a reason for denying access to classified information:

> The United States Government does not discriminate on the basis of race, color, religion, sex, national origin, disability, or sexual orientation in granting access to classified information.

Under the 1981 policy on homosexuality, one of the reasons cited for denying homosexuals entrance into the military was "to prevent breaches of security." With the enactment of the 1993 law, references to security concerns were removed. In a 1994 letter to Senator John H. Chafee, Assistant Secretary of Defense Emmett Paige, Jr. wrote:

---

[37] See H. R. 3396, Representative Barr, May 7, 1996, and S. 1740, Senator Nickles, May 8, 1996.

[38] P. L. 104-199.

> DOD is in full agreement with the [General Accounting Office] and the Attorney General that sexual orientation may not be used as a basis for or negative factor in determining a person's eligibility for a security clearance. However, sexual conduct, whether heterosexual or homosexual, may be considered in clearance or access determinations if such conduct reasonably raises a question as to character, judgment, stability, candor, or indirect susceptibility to coercion, duress, undue influence, pressure or compromise.
>
> DOD's current adjudicative guidelines do not include homosexual orientation as a potentially disqualifying condition for a security clearance. Rather, both the current DOD adjudicative guidelines and the common adjudicative guidelines that are under consideration, focus on conduct, concealment and coercion as relevant factors in security clearance decisions, regardless of sexual orientation.

The DOD Directives for implementing the statue enacted in November 1993 contain a section on Personnel Security which stated:

> Policy concerning personnel security investigations is also changed to provide that no investigations or inquiries will be conducted solely to determine an individual's sexual orientation, and that questions pertaining to an individual's sexual orientation will not be asked on personnel security questionnaires. Investigations will be limited to questions concerning sexual conduct – either homosexual or heterosexual – or concerning concealment of sexual conduct or orientation.
>
> Investigations into allegations of sexual conduct or concealment will proceed only if the sexual conduct or concealment gives rise to a legitimate security concern under the applicable standards. The new policy specifies that an individual's efforts to follow DOD policy on homosexual conduct in the Armed Forces by not openly acknowledging his or her homosexual orientation do not constitute concealment.

Finally, the new policy makes clear that information about homosexual orientation or conduct obtained during a security clearance investigation will not be used by the Military Departments in separation proceedings.

According to a December 1993 Memorandum entitled "Changes to Defense Investigative Manual – Sexual Conduct."

> No investigations or inquiries will be conducted solely to determine a subject's sexual orientation. Investigators are not to ask direct questions about sexual orientation unless credible, relevant information has been developed from other sources. Investigators should not ask questions unless the individual introduces the matter or it is developed through other sources.[39]

Further, according to a General Accounting Office (GAO) report, the 1993 Defense Investigative Service Manual for Personnel Security Investigations:

> These procedures are applicable to investigations of civilian and contractor personnel. Under certain circumstances (e. g., sexual acts, conduct, or behavior include acts performed with a minor, involving coercion, force, or violence, or acts committed for money), investigators can expand an investigation, but investigations or inquiries will not be conducted solely to determine an individual's sexual orientation.
>
> Allegations of an individual's sexual conduct should be designed to elicit information that adjudicative authorities consider in accordance with clearance denial criteria. DOD's current definition of "moral conduct" includes sexual conduct which may or may not be technically illegal in any given jurisdiction.[40]

---

[39] U. S. General Accounting Office. Security Clearances: Consideration of Sexual Orientation in the Clearance Process, GAO/NSIAD-95-21, March 1995: 9.

[40] GAO: 9.

GAO noted that DOD officials told them that investigators no longer use this definition of "moral conduct."

Finally, current DOD guidelines treat concealment as a security concern. According to GAO, coworkers and family members must be informed by the individual of the applicant's homosexual "orientation," if a claim of nonconcealment is to be supported. It is expected that DOD has or will soon revise its guidelines to eliminate this language. This language is most problematic under "don't ask, don't tell." Individuals are not allowed to "tell their homosexual orientation." However, concealment could result in a denial of a clearance. Conversely, if a person does not tell and does not engage in homosexual acts, as required by law, the entire issue is moot. Investigators, who cannot ask, will have no information that leads them to believe the person is concealing his or her homosexuality. This raises the questions whether any such revision is needed in the first place. Critics contend that any revision will arguably serve only to protect individuals who have already broken DOD rules. Conversely, it is expected that these guidelines will be revised in order to make them consistent with current law and regulations. GAO noted that prior to 1991, 16 cases of security clearance decisions involving homosexuality were made by DOD involving civilians or contract employees. Of these, eight clearances were revoked because the individuals concealed their sexual "orientation." Taking into consideration that 6 million clearance and access decisions have been entered into the Defense Clearance and Investigation Index, these eight cases represent an extraordinarily small proportion of the total.

According to data collected by GAO, 1,945 security clearances were denied, revoked, or suspended in FY1993 by DOD for any reason. Army, Navy, and Air Force records accounted for 954 of these. Using haphazard sampling techniques (i. e., not scientific), GAO found that for other agencies (including civilians at the Defense Mapping Agency), only 9 cases out of 129 cited factors in security clearance actions related to sexual misconduct (including one case categorized as "sexual misconduct/drugs"). To extrapolate from these questionable data, approximately 67 DOD personnel would have had their clearances denied, revoked, or suspended, based on sexual misconduct if this rage held across agencies.

There are reasons to believe that this extrapolation represents an overestimate. First, prior to 1993, DOD barred open homosexuality. Since then, "don't ask, don't tell" has been in effect. These rules would serve to discourage individuals from joining the military or, once in, discourage them from allowing their sexuality to become an issue. Second, as far back as the 1950s, individuals were to be discharged on the basis of homosexuality,, and not as security problems unless there existed an explicit security issue. Without criminal charges, commanders could avoid many problems by taking the administrative route of discharging open homosexuals. Last, there has been at least one case of an individual entering the military and being allowed to reenlist numerous times despite his acknowledgment of being a homosexual and despite routine security investigations. Thus, even if an individual was known to be a homosexual and was subjected to security clearance investigations, it was not assured that he or she would be discharged.

By issuing his Executive Order, the President has arguably removed the homosexuality issue from consideration in the security clearance process. However, the impact of the order on DOD security clearances is still uncertain. Questions can be raised concerning what "inferences" would justify a more thorough investigation. Conversely, how would this language dissuade investigators when "inferences" exist that could lead to discovery of UCMJ violations? Ultimately, this is a matter of professional interpretation by those investigating and adjudicating cases.

TITLE IX AND SCHOOL DISTRICT LIABILITY FOR STUDENT-ON-STUDENT SEXUAL HARASSMENT: *DAVIS V. MONROE COUNTY BOARD OF EDUCATION*

Kimberly D. Jones

In *Davis v. Monroe County Board of Education*, the U.S. Supreme Court, in a 5-4 decision, addressed the issue of liability of a school district for student-on-student sexual harassment. The case was brought under Title IX of the Education Amendments of 1972, which prohibits discrimination on the basis of sex in educational programs or activities that receive federal funding. The Court held that the school district is liable under "[a] private Title IX damages action...only where the funding recipient is deliberately indifferent to sexual harassment, of which the recipient has actual knowledge, and that harassment is so severe, pervasive, and objectively offensive that it can be said to deprive the victims of access to the educational opportunities or benefits provided by the school."

The U.S. Supreme Court has decided the standard of liability that courts should apply in determining whether a school district should be held responsible for monetary damages for student-on-student sexual harassment. Justice O'Connor, writing for the majority in *Davis v. Monroe County Board of Education*, held that "[a] private Title IX damages action may lie against a school board in cases of student-on-student harassment, but only where the funding recipient is deliberately indifferent to sexual harassment, of which the recipient has actual knowledge, and that harassment is so severe, pervasive, and objectively offensive that it can be said to deprive the victims of access to the educational opportunities or benefits provided by the school."[1]

The case began when Aurelia Davis sued in federal district court, on behalf of her daughter LaShonda, against the Monroe County Board of Education and two school officials. The Davis' alleged that the school district and the named school officials violated Title IX of the Education Amendments of 1972 by failing to prevent a fellow student from sexually harassing LaShonda. Davis' suit sought $500,000 in compensatory and punitive damages.

Title IX of the Education Amendments of 1972 prohibits discrimination on the basis of sex in educational programs or activities receiving federal funding. In *Franklin v. Gwinnett County Public Schools,* the Court held that the sexual harassment of a student by a teacher was discrimination based on sex and, therefore, a violation of the anti-discrimination mandate of Title IX.[2] The Court has also held that there is an implied private right of action under Title IX,[3] and that monetary damages may be recovered.[4] During its 1997 term, the Court decided *Gebser v. Lago Vista Independent School District*, which held that a school district is not liable for sexual harassment of a student by a teacher, "unless an official of the school district who at a minimum has authority to institute corrective measures on the district' s behalf has actual notice of, and is deliberately indifferent to, the teacher's misconduct."[5]

LaShonda Davis alleges that during her 5th grade year, she was subjected to at least eight incidents of sexual harassment committed by a male student, G. F., who was in several of her classes.[6] She allegedly reported these

---

[1] No. 97-843, slip op. at 1 (U. S. May 24, 1999). For a general overview of sexual harassment in education see CRS Report 98-798, *Sexual Harassment in Education: Recent Legal Development Under Title IX of the Education Amendments of 1972*, by Kimberly D. Jones.

[2] 503 U. S. 60, 75 (1992).

[3] Cannon v. University of Chicago, 441 U. S. 677 (1979).

[4] Franklin v. Gwinnett County Public Schools, 503 U. S. 60 (1992).

[5] Gebser v. Lago Vista Independent School Dist., 524 U. S. 274, 118 S. Ct. 1989, 1993 (1998). See also CRS Report , *Title IX and School District Liability for Sexual Harassment by a Teacher: Gebser v. Lago Vista Independent School District*, by Kimberly D. Jones.

[6] No. 97-843, slip op. at 2 (U. S. May 24, 1999). "According to the petitioner's complaint, the harassment began in December 1992, when the classmate, G. F., attempted to touch LaShonda's

incidents to three of her teachers, to the school's principal, and to her mother. In addition, Aurelia Davis complained to the school principal and to two teachers about the incidents. Davis alleged that LaShonda's grades dropped, and she threatened suicide because of the harassing behavior. The Davis' argued that the school did not take appropriate action to end the harassment. The harassment stopped when the male student was charged with, and pleaded guilty to, sexual battery.

The Davis' complaint was dismissed by the district court, but on appeal was reinstated by a three judge panel of the 11th Circuit. The school board sought a rehearing of the decision before the full panel of the 11th Circuit. The full panel framed the issue as whether Davis' "allegations describe an injury for which the law provides relief."[7] Ultimately, the full panel reversed the three-judge panel and dismissed Davis' Title IX claim. The Davis' appealed to the Supreme Court which granted the appeal and heard oral argument on January 12, 1999.

SUMMARY OF U.S. SUPREME COURT DECISION IN *DAVIS V. MONROE COUNTY BOARD OF EDUCATION*

Justice O'Connor, writing for the majority, framed the issue in *Davis* as "whether, and under what circumstances, a recipient of federal educational funds can be liable [under Title IX] in a private damages action arising from student-on-student sexual harassment.[8] Title IX states in relevant part that, "No person in the United States, shall, on the basis of sex, be excluded from participation in, be denied the benefits of, or be subjected to discrimination under any education program or activity receiving Federal financial

breasts and genital area and made vulgar statements such as 'I want to get in bed with you' and 'I want to feel your boobs.'...G. F.'s conduct allegedly continued for many months. In early February, G. F. purportedly placed a door stop in his pants and proceeded to act in a sexually suggestive manner toward LaShonda during physical education class...In mid-April 1993, G. F. allegedly rubbed his body against LaShonda in the school hallway in what LaShonda considered a sexually suggestive manner..." *Id.* At 2-3.

[7] 120 F.3d 1390, 1393 (11th Cir. 1997), *rev'd,*___U.S.___, No.97-843, slip op. (U.S. May 24, 1999).

[8] No. 97-843, slip op. at 6.

assistance...."[9] "Congress authorized an administrative enforcement scheme for Title IX. Federal departments or agencies...may rely on 'any...means authorized by law,' including termination of funding to give effect to the statue's restrictions."[10]

Justice O'Connor notes that Title IX was enacted pursuant to Congress' power under the Spending Clause of the U.S. Constitution.[11] O'Connor points out that the spending clause creates a quasi-contract because the recipient agrees to accept certain conditions in exchange for the receipt of federal funds. Therefore, O'Connor reasons that "private damages actions are available only where recipients of federal funding had adequate notice that they could be liable for the conduct at issue."[12] According to the majority's opinion, "Congress [must] speak with a clear voice,' recognizing that ' [t]here can, of course, be no knowing acceptance [of the terms of the putative contract] if a State is unaware of the conditions [imposed by the legislation] or is unable to ascertain what is expected of it."[13]

The school board argued that Title IX did not provide adequate notice that it could be held liable for student-on-student sexual harassment and that Title IX only applies to the actions of the grant recipient, not third parites.[14] Furthermore, the Board argued that it should not be held liable for the acts of a third party which it had little control over. Justice O'Connor disagreed with the board, finding that Davis was not suing the Board over the actions of the alleged harasser, but over the Board's "own decision to remain idle in the face of know student-on-student harassment in its schools."[15]

First, O'Connor points out that the administrative enforcement of Title IX "has long provided funding recipients with notice that they may be liable for their failure to respond to the discriminatory acts of certain non-agents."[16] Moreover, the Court notes that "common law...has put schools on notice that

---

[9] 20 U. S. C. A. § 1681 (West 1990 & Supp. 1998).
[10] No. 97-843, slip op. at 7.
[11] U. S. Const. Art. I, § 8, cl. 1.
[12] *Id.* at 8-9.
[13] *Id.* at 9 (quoting Pennhurst State School and Hospital v. Halderman, 451 U. S. 1, 24-25 (1981)).
[14] *Id.* at 9.
[15] *Id.* at *10.*
[16] *Id.* at 12.

they may be held responsible under state law for their failure to protect students from the tortuous acts of third parties."[17]

The Court opined that the school board, standing in its "custodial" role, had authority over the environment in which the harassment occurred.[18] In this case, the harassment took place "during school hours and on school grounds."[19] The majority then concluded "that recipients of federal funding may be liable for 'subject[ing]' their students to discrimination where the recipient is deliberately indifferent to know acts of student-on-student sexual harassment and the harasser is under the school's disciplinary authority."[20] The Court's holding stresses that it is not meant to dictate the type of discipline that schools must use and urges lower courts to "refrain from second guessing the disciplinary decision of school administrators."[21] To ensure this, the majority states that the decision of school administrators will not be disturbed unless their "response to the harassment or lack thereof is clearly unreasonable in light of the known circumstances."[22] The Court noted that "[A] university might not, for example, be expected to exercise the same degree of control over its students that a grade school would enjoy...and it would be entirely reasonable for a school to refrain from a form of disciplinary action that would expose it to constitutional or statutory claims."[23]

O'Connor notes that Title IX "does not bar...private damages action under Title IX where the funding recipient engages in intentional conduct that violates the clear terms of the statute."[24] Relying on its decision in *Gebser*, the Court notes that a school district would not be liable for teacher-student harassment unless the school board had actual knowledge of the harassment and was deliberately indifferent. According to O'Connor, the "deliberate indifference" standard "sought to eliminate any 'risk that the recipient would be liable in damages not for its own official decision but instead for its employees' independent actions.'"[25]

---

[17] *Id.* at 13.
[18] *Id.*
[19] *Id.*at 15.
[20] *Id.* at 16.
[21] *Id.* at 17.
[22] *Id.*at 17.
[23] *Id.* at *18*.
[24] *Id.* at 11.
[25] *Id.* at 11 (quoting Gebser v. Lago Vista Indep. Sch. Dist., 524 U. S. 274, 290-291).

O'Connor also relied on the *Gebser* decision in reiterating the Court's refusal to apply agency principles to Title IX, generally, and student-on-student sexual harassment specifically. Referring to the language of Title IX, which unlike Title VII, does not define or refer to "agents," the Court concluded that recognition of agency principles under Title IX "would conflict with the Spending Clauses's notice requirement and Title IX's express administrative enforcement scheme."[26]

Justice O'Connor reasoned that a standard similar to the one established in *Gebser* could be applied to peer sexual harassment cases. "If a funding recipient does not engage in harassment directly, it may not be liable for damages unless its deliberate indifference 'subject[s]' its students to harassment. That is, the deliberate indifference must, at a minimum, 'cause [students] to undergo' harassment or 'make them liable or vulnerable' to it."[27] These factors are interpreted by O'Connor "to limit a recipient's damages liability to circumstances wherein the recipient exercises substantial control over both the harasser and the context in which the known harassment occurs."[28]

After applying the deliberate indifference standard to student-on-student sexual harassment, Justice O'Connor then turned to the definition of discrimination "in the context of a private damages action."[29] O'Connor concluded that "funding recipients are properly held liable in damages only where they are deliberately indifferent to sexual harassment, of which they have actual knowledge, that is so severe, pervasive, and objectively offensive that it can be said to deprive the victims to access to the educational opportunities or benefits provided by the school."[30] The majority further defines discrimination as "behavior...serious enough to have the systemic effect of denying the victim equal access to an educational program or activity."[31] Some factors the Court finds compelling are "the ages of the harasser and the victim and the number of individuals involved."[32] The Court

[26] *Id.* at 8.
[27] *Id.* at 13.
[28] *Id.* at 14.
[29] *Id.* at 19.
[30] *Id.* at 19-20. "Whether gender-oriented conduct rises to the level of actionable "harassment" thus depends on a constellation of surrounding circumstances, expectations, and relationships." *Id.* at 20 (quoting Oncale v. Sundowner Offshore Services, inc., 523 U. S. 75, 82 (1998).
[31] *Id.* at 22.
[32] *Id.* at 20.

explicitly notes "[d]amages are not available for simple acts of teasing and name-calling among school children...even where thee comments target differences in gender."[33]

The Court overturned the decision of the 11th Circuit Court of Appeals and reinstated the Davis' Title IX claim. While the Court could not gauge whether Davis could meet the standards articulated, it did point to several allegations to support reinstating her claim. O'Connor referred to her allegations of "repeated acts of sexual harassment," multiple victims, and the "negative effect on her daughter's ability to receive an education."[34] The Court also noted out that there was support for the conclusion that G. F.'s actions were severe, pervasive, and objectively offensive, and that Davis warranted an opportunity to "show both actual knowledge and deliberate indifference on the part of the Board, which made no effort whatsoever either to investigate or to put an end to the harassment."[35]

Justice Kennedy, wrote the dissenting opinion which was joined by Chief Justice Rehnquist, and Associate Justices Scalia and Thomas. Kennedy argued that "[s]chools cannot be held liable for peer sexual harassment because Title IX does not give them clear and unambiguous notice that they are liable in damages for failure to remedy discrimination by their students."[36] First, Kennedy points out that legislation enacted pursuant to the Spending Clause is in the nature of a contract and that under previous decisions recipients are entitled to clear notice of the contract terms.[37] Secondly, Kennedy cautions the Court about fashioning private damages remedies under Title IX, since the private right of action is imposed judicially, not statutorily.[38] Next, Kennedy finds that nothing in the language of Title IX or its regulations provides clear, unambiguous notice that a recipient may be held liable for monetary damages for student-on-student sexual harassment.[39] Kennedy also criticizes the majority's rejection of using agency principles as a guide for liability.

---

[33] *Id.* at 21.
[34] *Id.* at 23.
[35] *Id.* at 23.
[36] No. 97-843, slip op. at 5 (Kennedy, J., dissenting).
[37] *Id.* at 3.
[38] *Id.*
[39] *Id.* 7.

The dissent criticizes the majority's standards as unclear and therefore violative of the Spending Clause's clear notice requirement.[40] For example, the dissent notes that, unlike in *Gebser*, the majority did not indicate "the type of school employee who must know about the harassment before it is actionable."[41] Kennedy also takes issue with defining the behavior of typically immature youngsters as "sexual harassment" and "gender discrimination."[42] The dissent emphasizes that "Schools are not workplaces and children are not adults," and the Court should not apply principles that have been used in the workplace to schools.[43] Ultimately, the dissent concludes that the majority's standard will result in a flood of lawsuits and divert funds away from educational institutions.[44]

---

[40] *Id.* at 19. "The majority thus imposes on schools potentially crushing financial liability for student conduct that is not prohibited in clear terms by Title IX and that cannot, even after today's opinion, be identified by either schools or courts with any precision." *Id.*

[41] *Id.* at 27.
[42] *Id.* at 21.
[43] *Id.* at 22.
[44] *Id.* at 27.

TITLE IX AND SEX DISCRIMINATION IN EDUCATION": AN OVERVIEW

Gary L. Galemore

Title IX was enacted on June 23, 1972, as part of a general education bill, the Education Amendments of 1972.[1] It prohibits discrimination on the basis of sex in federally assisted education programs or activities. The word "programs" under Title IX refers to all of the activities of any educational institution receiving federal funding for any part of its program, a point clarified by Congress under the Civil Rights Restoration Act of 1988.[2] Numerous school activities fall under the umbrella of Title IX. It applies to admissions, recruitment, financial aid, academic programs, student treatment and services, counseling and guidance, discipline classroom assignment, grading, vocational education, recreation, physical education, housing, employment, and athletics.

An educational institution is defined as any "public or private pre-school, elementary or secondary school or any institution of vocational, professional or higher education."

Enforcement and administration of Title IX is primarily the responsibility of the Office of Civil Rights (OCR) at the Department of Education (DOE). Administrative complaints concerning possible Title IX violations may be filed with this office. A complaint to the Office of Civil Rights is not a

---

[1] PL. 92-318; 86 Stat. 373, 1972: 42 U.S.C. 906a.

[2] PL. 100-259; 102 Stat. 28, 1988: 20 U.S.C. 1681 et seq.

lawsuit. A complaint can be filed by anyone: a parent, a student athlete, a team, or even a concerned third party. The OCR does not file lawsuits on behalf of persons or groups injured by alleged discrimination. It can, but rarely does, seek to have federal financial assistance withheld from educational institutions not in compliance with Title IX. The OCR's first choice of action is the alleged victim and the school. A commonly expressed misunderstanding about the OCR is that it directly disperses federal funds to schools to implement Title IX or conduct sports programs, and that this money can be withdrawn.

Contrary to this perception, the OCRT neither has appropriated federal funds available to disperse for sports programs, nor is the agency authorized to do so by law. Federal financial assistance that can be withheld can take many forms. It can be defined as federal grants or loans to educational institutions for acquisitions, construction, renovations, restorations, or repairs of buildings and facilities. Federal assistance can also take the form of scholarships, loans, grants, wages, or other funding extended to a school directly or through students at the school. In addition, it can take the form of federal surplus property, either donated or sold to a school, or services provided by federal personnel. Contracts, agreements, or other arrangements between education institutions or individuals associated with educational institutions and federal agencies, such as defense-related research conducted by an educational institution for the Department of the Army, can also be regarded as federal financial assistance for the purposes of Title IX. An educational institution may lose its federal financial assistance if it is found to be in non-compliance with Title IX.

Although the federal government is responsible for Title IX enforcement and may terminate funding on the basis of sex bias, few educational institutions have lost funding for this reason. Thus far in Title IX's almost 20-year history, pressure for stronger enforcement has come largely as a result of court suits initiated by women's groups, rather than through agency action. In 1979, the U. S. Supreme Court held that an individual has an implied private right of action under Title IX, allowing for a judicially-imposed remedy. In other words, claimants may sue in court for alleged discriminatory practices. This decision opened, in addition to the procedures in place at the Office of Civil Rights, and entirely new avenue for redressing alleged sexual harassment and gender bias claims, and has resulted in dozens of court challenges under Title IX. Maybe even more significantly, in 1992, the

Supreme Court ruling in *Franklin v. Gwinnett County* allowed for monetary awards against educational institutions found to be intentionally discriminating.[3]

Title IX grew out of the women's civil rights movement of the late 1960s and early 1970s. In that period, Congress began to focus attention on systemic educational barriers to women and girls, in part because of the associated limitation on women's employment opportunities, which led to lower lifetime earnings and fewer opportunities generally.[4] This problem had serious implications, not only for women themselves, but also for their ability to contribute to their families, to society, and to the national economy. Hearings in June and July of 1970, prior to passage of Title IX, documented what supporters perceived as pervasive discrimination and sex stereotyping in the treatment of males and females in educational institutions. These hearings and other investigations gave impetus to the growing effort to make taxpayer funded educational programs more equitable.[5]

Although Title IX has been on the statute books for almost 30 years, the law is considered by many to be only a partial success. For persons directly affected by Title IX, the law remains confusing and almost always controversial. To this day, the public perception of the intended purpose and major impact of Title IX is in its application to women's athletics, yet the statue applies to every area of sex-based discrimination in an educational setting.[6]

---

[3] 503 U. S. 60 (1992).

[4] Since the Supreme Court decisions in *Brown v. Board of Education* (347 U. S. 583 [1954]), the relationship between equality in education and in society has been the object of public concern. In fact, Title IX is based on Title VI of the Civil Rights Act of 1964 (P. L. 88-352, 78 Stat. 252), which prohibits discrimination on the basis or race, color, or national origin in federally assisted programs, except that Title IX does not exclude employment form coverage of the statute.

[5] U. S. Congress, House Special Subcommittee on Education, Discrimination Against Women, hearings on Sec. 805 of H. R. 16098, 91st Cong., 2nd sess., 1970 (Washington: GPO, 1970).

[6] Several agencies and activities are exempt from Title IX, including educational institutions operated or controlled by religious organizations, if application of Title IX would be inconsistent with the religious tenets of those organizations. Title IX is not applicable to federal military and merchant marine academies. Social fraternities and sororities whose members are primarily students at institutions of higher education are exempt from Title IX. So are voluntary youth organizations which are tax-exempt and/or whose membership is traditionally limited to one sex. These organizations include groups such as the Boy Scouts of America, the Girls Scouts of America, the Young Men's Christian Association, and the Camp Fire Girls.

WHY CONGRESS ENACTED TITLE IX

The testimony before congressional committees prior to passage of Title IX in 1970 documented examples of differential treatment of males and females.[7] Examples from the testimony included the following:

- Some publicly-funded universities did not admit women to undergraduate programs, had higher admissions standards for women than men, or had imposed sex-based quotas.

- Certain academic programs and courses within publicly-funded educational institutions, such as nursing schools, would not admit married women.

- Equally qualified women were found to be less likely to receive financial aid or to receive smaller amounts than their male counterparts, and married women often were excluded from receiving awards of financial aid.

- Some school-sponsored activities, such as honor societies, were reserved for male students only, and women's athletics were commonly funded at levels far below parallel programs for men.

- Women frequently were discouraged from applying to law and medical schools or majoring in hard sciences, such as physics or engineering.

- Women who sought employment at educational institutions with equivalent training and experience to that of male applicants were often hired at lower salaries than their male counterparts and were less likely to be promoted to principal, department head, dean, or university president.

---

[7] Ibid., passim.

- In high school and college athletics, few women were allowed to coach athletics or hold administrative positions in athletic departments. In 1971, approximately 295,000 girls participated in highs cool sports, and only about 25, 000 played sports at the college level.

CHANGES ATTRIBUTED TO TITLE IX IN INCREASING EQUAL EDUCATIONAL OPPORTUNITY

Proponents of Title IX contend that a more equal, more educated, and more prosperous nation has resulted because of the far-reaching effects of this legislation. While no definitive study has been made of the full impact of Title IX, there are a number of indicators of substantial change. For example:

- In colleges and universities, women now constitute majorities in college enrollment and completion of a degree, and are the majority of recipients of master's degrees. In 1971, only 18% of young women completed four or more years of college, compared with 26% of young men. By 2006, women are projected to earn 55% of all bachelor's degrees.

- In graduate and professional fields, women have had new opportunities to advance and broaden their education, and have made significant progress in specialty fields. In 1999, women earned nearly 50% of all U.S. medical degrees, compared with 1972, when only 9% of medical school degrees went to women. Women also earned 39% of all dental degrees in 1994; in 1972 they were only 1% of the graduates. In 1994, women accounted for 43% of all law school degrees, up from 7% in 1972. OF all doctoral degrees awarded in 1994, 44% went to women, compared with 25% with 25% in 1977.

- There are more female faculty members now than in 1972, with women constituting about 38% of faculty members at two-year public colleges, and almost 20% at private four-year colleges and universities. In 1972, women held 10% of all academic positions.

- In athletics, an area that has received the largest share of media and public attention, women's participation has increased markedly since 1971, with more than 135,000 women presently competing in intercollegiate sports. Women currently constitute nearly 40% of all college athletes, compared with 15% in 1972. Recent data show that approximately 2.6 million high school girls participate in a wide selection of high school sports, representing nearly 40% of all high school athletes. In 1971, only 294,000, or 7.5%, of high school athletes were female. Female participation in sports, like receiving a college education, has had unexpected benefits for women. Studies have shown that values learned from sports participation, such as teamwork, leadership, discipline, and pride in accomplishment, are important attributes as women increase their participation in the workforce, as well as their entry into business management and ownership positions in ever higher numbers. For example, 80% of female managers of Fortune 500 companies have a sports background. Also, high school girls who participate in team sports have been found to be less likely to drop out of school, smoke, drink alcohol, or have unwanted pregnancies.

CONTINUING CONTROVERSIES

One of the reasons for the seemingly disproportionate attention paid to women's athletics under Title IX relates in no small part to persistent differences in funding support for men's and women's sports programs (a more easily measured indicator than classroom inequities). Although women represent the majority of total students in undergraduate college programs and nearly 40% of all athletics, a 1997 gender-equity study by the National Collegiate Athletic Association (NCAA)[8] found that spending for men's athletics continues to dwarf monies spent on women's sports, specifically $2.4 million per school on average for men versus $663,000 on average for women.

Although the sport of football accounts for a substantial portion of this disparity, and even though some specific universities and colleges reportedly are doing a good job of balancing their sports programs, critics would say much more needs to be done in this area.

For some, the current gains made by female athletes under Title IX represent sufficient progress. They believe that a more aggressive implementation of Title IX would result in even more men's non-revenue generating sports (such as wrestling) being dropped by educational institutions in order to add mandated women's teams to meet the equity standards of the Act.[9]

These opponents of Title IX point to the sports administrators at colleges and universities selectively dropping men's teams as an unintended consequence of Title IX enforcement. They contend that the law has resulted in a kind of reverse discrimination against men's sports programs, substituting discrimination against men for discrimination against women, and thus defeating the original intent of the law.[10] They also point to the fact that as women's enrollment at colleges and universities continues to grow, making women a majority of the student body, it becomes more difficult to meet the law's requirement for proportionate athletic programs. Many opponents have

[8] National Collegiate Athletic Association, *NCAA Gender-Equity Study: Summary of Results.* (Overland Park, KS: April 1997).

[9] Amy Shipley, "Title IX at 25," *Washington Post*, July 6, 1997, pp. A1, A6-7.

[10] Under Title IX, a school is considered in compliance with the gender-equity requirements of the statute if it meets one prong of a three-pronged test: if the ratio of female athletes to male athletes is substantially proportionate to the ratio of female students to male students; if the college or university can show that it is making a good faith effort to balance its programs over time or in a reasonable number of years; or if the educational institution can show that there are no unmet sports needs (interests) among the under-represented class, which is usually, but not always, women. Determining if needs are being met can be accomplished by surveying the student body for its opinions or by noting the number of club sports at the institution as a measure of student interests in varsity versions of those sports.

also suggested that the problems with compliance could be simplified by removing football from the equation.

For advocates of Title IX, however, the perceived slow progress in implementing gender equity not only is harmful, but also contravenes the legal requirements of the law. They believe that educational institutions must adapt to the needs and legal rights of both male and female students, and must serve the entire student population, rather than, in the case of athletes, concentrating limited resources on a few high-profile sports like football and basketball.

They also argue that Title IX has been the law since 1972, but only in the last 10 years have schools made an honest effort to meet the requirements of the law, and 30 years is sufficient time to bring athletic programs into compliance. Supporters of greater enforcement of Title IX reject opponents' arguments that men's football and basketball are revenue-producing sports and, thus, should not be included in formulas seeking to achieve equity. This argument includes the proposition that men's football and basketball programs are critical to supporting all other no-revenue sports at most institutions.

Proponents do not entirely disagree with this pleading, but point out that over 40% of NCAA Division I schools are losing money on their sports departments, even with football and basketball. Advocates of Title IX also content that these revenue sports not only raise greater profits that most other sports played at the college level, as claimed, but also consume a greater share of limited funds.

TITLE IX AND SCHOOL DISTRICT LIABILITY FOR SEXUAL HARASSMENT BY A TEACHER: GEBSER V. LAGO VISTA INDEPENDENT SCHOOL DISTRICT

Kimberly Jones

BACKGROUND

The U.S. Supreme Court recently decided the standard of liability that courts should apply in determining whether a school district should be held responsible for damages when a teacher sexually harasses a student. Justice O'Connor, writing for the majority in *Gebser v. Lago Vista Independent School District,*[1] held that "damages may not be recovered [under Title IX for the sexual harassment of a student by one of the district's teachers]...unless an official of the school district who at a minimum has authority to institute corrective measures on the district's behalf has actual notice of, and is deliberately indifferent to, the teacher's misconduct."[2]

Alida Gebser and her parents brought a sexual harassment lawsuit against Alida's high school teacher, Frank Waldrop, after it was discovered that Alida and Waldrop were having a sexual relationship. Waldrop established a relationship with Gebser while she was an eighth grader and a member of a

---

[1] Gebser v. Lago Vista Independent School Dist., 522 U.S._____, 118 S. Ct. 1989, 1993 (1998)

high school book discussing group taught by Waldrop. When Gebser began high school she was assigned to classes taught by Waldrop who often made sexually suggestive comments to Gebser and other students. He initiated the sexual relationship with Gebser while visiting her home on the pretense of delivering a book. In 1992, the parents of two other students complained to the principal about Waldrop's suggestive comments and Waldrop apologized and said it would not happen again. Waldrop received a warning from the principal, but the school district's superintendent who was also the district's Title IX coordinator, was never notified of the incident. Gebser never informed anyone, including her parents, about her relationship with Waldrop and Gebser's name did not come up in regard to the complaint. Gebser and Waldrop's relationship continued with the two often having sexual intercourse during class time, but not on school property. The relationship ended after they were discovered by police. Waldrop was criminally prosecuted, fired from his teaching position, and had his teaching license revoked by the state.

Gebser and her parents brought suit in state court against the Lago Vista School District and Waldrop. The suit alleged a violation of Title IX of the Education Amendments of 1972 and sought compensatory and punitive damages.[3] The case was moved to federal district court and summary judgment was granted in favor of the Lago Vista School District. The only issue on appeal was the dismissal of the Title IX claim. The 5th Circuit Court of Appeals affirmed the lower court decision holding that "School districts are not liable in tort for teacher-student harassment under Title IX unless an employee who has been invested by the school board with supervisory power over the offending employee actually knew of the abuse, had the power to end the abuse, and failed to do so."[4]

SUMMARY OF U.S. SUPREME COURT DECISION IN *GEBSER V. LAGO VISTA INDEPENDENT SCHOOL DISTRICT*

Title IX states in relevant part that, "No person in the United States, shall, on the basis of sex, be excluded from participation in, be denied the benefits

---

[2] Gebesr, 118 S. Ct. at 1993.

[3] 20 U.S.C.A. § 1681 (West 1990 & Supp. 1998).

[4] 106 F .3d 1226 (5th Cir. 1997).

of, or be subjected to discrimination under any education program or activity receiving Federal financial assistance..."[5] The issue of sexual harassment was first addressed by the Court in the employment context. In *Meritor Sav. Bank, FSB v. Vinson,*[6] the Court held that "when a supervisor sexually harasses a subordinate because of the subordinate's sex, that supervisor discriminate[s] on the basis of sex."[7] Later, the Court in *Franklin v. Gwinnett County Public Schools,* relied on the rationale of *Vinson,* to find that when a student is sexually harassed by a teacher because of that student's sex, it is discrimination based on sex and violative of the anti-discrimination mandate of Title IX.[8] The Court has held in past decisions that there is an implied private right of action under Title IX[9] and that monetary damages may be recovered.[10] However, the question was left open as to what standard should apply to determine when damages should be awarded. The Gebsers urged the Court to apply the same standard of liability to a school district that it has applied to employers. In the employment context, the Court has applied principles of agency law where the employer may be held responsible for the acts of its agent, i.e. employee, when that agent is performing his official duties.[11] Employers may be held liable even if they are unaware of the employee's acts. The Gebsers argued that "in light of [*Franklin v. Gwinnett County Public School's*] comparison of teacher-student harassment with supervisor –employee harassment, agency principles should likewise apply in Title IX actions."[12]

The Gebsers evince two standards that the Court should apply when determining whether damages should lie under Title IX when determining whether damages should lie under Title IX when a teacher harasses a student. The first is the *respondeat superior* standard that would hold the school district liable "whenever a teacher's authority over a student facilitates the harassment."[13] Liability would exist regardless of whether the school district

---

[5] 20 U.S.C.A. § 1681.
[6] 477 U.S. 57 (1986).
[7] 477 U.S. at 64.
[8] 503 U.S. 60, 75 (1992).
[9] Cannon v. University of Chicago, 441 U.S. 677 (1979).
[10] Franklin v. Gwinnett County Public Schools, 503 U.S. 60 (1992).
[11] See Faragher v. City of Boca Raton, 522 U.S. ___(1998); Meritor Sav. Bank, FSB v. Vinson, 447 U.S. 57 (1986); Restatement (Second) of Agency § 219(2)(d) (1957).
[12] 118 S. Ct. at 1995.
[13] Id.

was aware of the harassment and regardless of any action the school district may take upon becoming aware. This is the same standard supported by the U.S. Department of Education and described in its 1997 Policy Guidance on Sexual Harassment.[14] In the alternative, the Gebsers argue that a school district should be liable "where the district knew or 'should have known' about the harassment but failed to uncover and eliminate it."[15] The Curt referred to this as the "consecutive notice" standard.

Justice O'Connor, writing for the majority, first addressed the Gebsers' attempt to apply principles established in sexual harassment cases brought under Title VII of the Civil Rights Act of 1964[16] to Title IX. First, Justice O'Connor found that the definition of "employer" in the Title VII included "any agent" of that employer, but similar language did not exist I Title IX. Second, the Court pointed out that unlike Title VII, Title IX does not contain an express cause of action, nor does it specifically provide for monetary damages. Justice O'Connor went on to say that because the private right of action in Title IX was implicit rather than explicit, the Court has great latitude in shaping an appropriate remedy. However, that remedy "must be reconciled with congressional purpose."[17] The Court determines congressional purpose by attempting to discern what Congress would have intended if the issue had been addressed when Title IX was enacted. The Court concluded that "it would 'frustrate the purposes' of Title IX to permit a damages recovery against a school district for a teacher's sexual harassment of a student based o principles of *respondeat superior* or constructive notice, i.e., without actual notice to a school district official."[18] The Court pointed to several factors to support its conclusion that "Congress did not intend to allow recovery in damages where liability rests solely on principles of vicarious liability or constructive notice."[19] Justice O'Connor compared Title VII and Title IX, since Title VII was the only civil rights statute in existence when Title IX was enacted. She noted that Title VII, as originally enacted, did not allow for recovery of monetary damages. Damages were later allowed under Title IX, but the amount of damages was capped. Instead, Justice O'Connor found that

---

[14] 62 Fed. Reg. 12034 (1997).

[15] 118 S. Ct. at 1995.

[16] 42 U.S.C.A. § 2000e et seq. (West 1994 & Supp. 1998)

[17] 118 S. Ct. at 1996.

[18] 118 S. Ct. at 1997.

[19] 118 S. Ct. at 1998.

Title IX was more analogous to Title VI of the Civil Rights Act. Title VI forbids discrimination based on race in programs receiving federal funding. The Court found that similar to Title VI, Title IX created a contract between the government and the recipient that the recipient would not discriminate. Further, Justice O'Connor concluded that "whereas Title VII aims centrally to compensate victims of discrimination, Title IX focuses more on 'protecting' individuals from discriminatory practices carried out by recipients of federal funds." The Court found that the contractual relationship of Title IX required that recipients of federal funds be on notice that they may be responsible for a monetary award. Justice O'Connor points out that the enforcement mechanism of Title IX requires actual notice to funding recipients and an opportunity to correct any violation. A reliance on agency principles would necessarily result in a recipient being held liable for acts they may not be aware of.[20] According to Justice O'Connor , Title IX's enforcement mechanism "Avoid[s] diverting education funding from beneficial uses where a recipient was unaware of discrimination in its programs and is willing to institute prompt corrective measures."[21] Justice O'Connor also noted that the penalty for a Title IX violation is loss of federal funding, while a damages award may exceed the amount of federal funds. Finally, Justice O'Connor concluded that [b]ecause the express remedial scheme under Title IX is predicated upon notice to an 'appropriate person' and an opportunity to rectify any violation, [the Court concludes], in the absence of further direction from Congress, that the implied damages remedy should be fashioned along the same lines."[22] An appropriate person must be "at a minimum, an official of the recipient entity with authority to take corrective action to end the discrimination."[23] If an appropriate person is notified of the discrimination, liability will lie only if the person responds "with deliberate indifference to discrimination." Deliberate indifference was described as, "an official decision by the recipient not to remedy the violation."[24] Applying this standard to the Gebsers' case, the plaintiff would not be entitled to monetary damages because an appropriate official was never notified. However, the Gebsers pointed out that Lago Vista never instituted a policy regarding the handling of sexual harassment claims as

---

[20] Id.
[21] 118 S. Ct. at 1999.
[22] Id.
[23] Id.
[24] 118 S. Ct. at 1999.

required by the Department of Education's regulations.[25] However, the Court found that the failure of Lago Vista to create a sexual harassment policy did not rise to the level of actual notice or deliberate indifference. Further, the Court found that the lack of a sexual harassment policy was not alone evidence of discrimination. However, the Department of Education would still be able to enforce the policy requirement administratively. Finally, the Court noted that this decision does not preclude a student from pursuing redress under any applicable state law.

Justice Stevens wrote a dissenting opinion which was joined by Justices Souter, Ginsburg, and Breyer.[26] Justice Stevens agreed with the majority that Title IX was analogous to Title VI, but disagreed that the lack of an explicit remedy in Title IX should act to limit liability for damages under the Act. Stevens noted that in the Court's previous decision in *Franklin*, the Court relied on the presumption that unless otherwise indicated "Congress intends to authorize 'all appropriate remedies.'"[27] Stevens also pointed to Congress' enactment of amendments to Title IX that indicate Congress' intent to not limit remedies available under Title IX.[29] Stevens also pointed out the Department of Education, the agency responsible for enforcing Title IX, has advocated this standard of liability. According to Justice Stevens,

> This case presents a paradigmatic example of a tort that was made possible, that was effected, and that was repeated over a prolonged period because of the powerful influence that Waldrop had over Gebser by reason of the authority that his employer, the school district, had delegated to him. As a secondary school teacher, Waldrop exercised even greater authority and control over his students than employers and supervisors exercise over their employees. His gross misuse of that authority allowed him to abuse his young student's trust.[30]

---

[25] 34 C.F.R. § 106.8(b) (1997).
[26] 118 S. Ct. at 2000-2007.
[27] 118 S. Ct. at 2001 (quoting Franklin v. Gwinnett County Public Schools, 503 U.S. 60, 66 (1992)).
[29] 118 S. Ct. at 2002.
[30] 118 S. Ct. at 2004.

Further, Stevens argues that the "Congress included the prohibition against discrimination on the basis of sex in Title IX to induce school boards to adopt and enforce practices that will minimize the danger that vulnerable students will be exposed to such odious behavior."[31] However, Stevens lamented that the rule adopted by the majority undermines this purpose since "school boards can insulate themselves from knowledge abut this sort of conduct" and escape liability.[32]

The dissent attacked the reasoning of the majority. First, Stevens dismissed the majority's look back at the Congress when Title IX was enacted and the limited remedies provided under civil rights law at that time, since the Court already had addressed that issue and held that remedies should be available under Title IX in it decision in *Franklin*.[33] Second, the dissent rejected the notion that the school district did not have adequate notice of a possible monetary award for a violation of Title IX because *Franklin* put school districts on notice. Finally, the dissent found inappropriate, the majority's reliance on the administrative scheme of Title IX and noted that the standard of the majority equates to no remedy under Title IX for student victims of sexual harassment.[34]

Justice Ginsburg wrote a separate dissenting opinion, which was joined by Justices Souter and Breyer. While Justice Ginsburg agreed with Justice Stevens' dissent, she argued that a school district should be able to use as an affirmative defense the fact that it has an effective and well-publicized policy on reporting and addressing sexual harassment. Ginsburg argued:

> The burden would be the school district's to show that its internal remedies were adequately publicized and likely would have provided redress without exposing the complainant to undue risk, effort, or expense. Under such regime, to the extent that a plaintiff unreasonably failed to avail herself of the school district's preventive and remedial measures, and consequently suffered avoidable harm. She would not qualify for Title IX relief.[35]

---

[31] Id.
[32] Id.
[33] 118 S. Ct. at 2005.
[34] Id.
[35] 118 S. Ct. at 2007.

The reaction to the *Gebser* decision has been mixed. Some have criticized the decision for creating too high a standard for alleged student-victims of sexual harassment.[36] U.S. Secretary of Education, Richard W. Riley issued a statement after the *Gebser* decision, that although a school district may not be liable for monetary damages for the sexual harassment of a student by a teacher, such behavior is still discrimination under Title IX, and federal education funding may be affected by such incidents.[37] However, the National School Boards Association (NSBA) and school districts across the country welcomed the Court's decision in *Gebser*. The NSBA filed a friend of the court brief on behalf of the Lago Vista School District arguing "that imposing a tougher standard would not deter similar harassment because school districts cannot predict this kind of behavior.[38]

---

[36] Lyle Denniston, *Limits Set On Sexual Suits*, The Baltimore Sun, June 23, 1998, at 1A; Jan Crawford Greenburg, *Top Court Shields Schools in Harassment Case,* Chicago Tribune, June 23, 1998, at 1.

[37] Statement By U.S. Secretary of Education Richard Riley, July 1, 1998.

[38] Jan Crawford Greenburg, *Top Court Shields Schools in Harassment Case,* Chicago Tribune, June 23, 1998, at 1; Mark Walsh, *High Court Limits District Liability on Harassment,* Education Week, June 24, 1998.

HOMOSEXUALITY AND THE FEDERAL CONSTITUTION: A LEGAL ANALYSIS OF THE U.S. SUPREME COURT RULING IN *ROMER V. EVANS*

Charles V. Dale

BACKGROUND

On November 3, 1992, Colorado voters approved Amendment 2, a referendum amending the state constitution. The amendment prohibited the state and its political subdivisions from adopting or enforcing any law, policy, or regulation that provided authority for claims of minority or protected status, quota preferences, or protection from discrimination to be based on "homosexual, lesbian or bisexual orientation."[1] The immediate effect of the referendum was to repeal local ordinances in Aspen, Boulder, and Denver prohibiting sexual orientation discrimination in employment, housing, and

---

[1] The amendment reads:

No protected Status Based on Homosexual, Lesbian, or Bisexual Orientation. Neither the State of Colorado, through any of its branches or departments, nor any of its agencies, political subdivisions, municipalities or school districts, shall enact, adopt or enforce any statute, regulation, ordinance, or policy whereby homosexual, lesbian or bisexual orientation, conduct, practices or relationships shall constitute or otherwise be the basis of or entitle any person or class of persons to have or claim any minority status, quota preferences, protected status or claim of discrimination. This Section of the Constitution shall be in all respects self-executing.

public accommodations, and an executive order by the Governor directing state agency-heads to "ensure non-discrimination" in hiring and promotion based on "sexual orientation," among other coverage grounds.[2] Significantly, the measure also foreclosed ordinary legislative channels to future gay rights lobbying efforts by, in effect, requiring proponents to achieve their goals through the state's constitutional amending process.

The Colorado trial and appellate courts each applied "strict scrutiny" Equal Protection review to condemn Amendment 2, but on the basis of somewhat differing rationales. In granting preliminary relief, state district court judge Bayliss strongly indicated that Amendment 2 would be found invalid unless justified by a "compelling" state interest because it infringed the "fundamental" right of an "independently identifiable group...not to have the state endorse and give effect to private biases." The Colorado State Supreme Court likewise invoked "fundamental rights" analysis as a basis for strictly scrutinizing the purpose and effects of the law, but differently conceived of the group right involved.[3] Thus, for Chief Justice Rovoira, the right to "equal participation in the political process" was "fundamental" under the Equal Protection Clause. The Colorado High Court rooted this right in precedents involving direct restrictions on the exercise of the right to vote, reappointment, candidate eligibility requirements, and other governmental attempts to limit the ability of certain groups to enact legislation through normal political processes.[4] As result, it was secured to all "independently identifiable

[2] Executive Order No. D0035 (Dec. 10, 1990)

[3] *Evans v. Romer*, 854 P. 2d 1270 (Colo.)(en banc)(issuing a temporary injunction), *cert. Denied*, 114 S. Ct 419 (1993).

[4] Specifically, the Colorado court pointed to U.S. Supreme Court ruling which had disapproved of popularly-inspired governmental restructuring to "fence out" or prevent minority groups from securing legislative favorable to their interests. In *Reitman v. Mulkey*, 387 U.S. 369 (1967), the Supreme Court disapproved a voter-initiated amendment to the California Constitution, known as Proposition 14, which repealed laws interfering with the sale or lease of private property and prevented their reenactment, since it would have created a constitutional right to discriminate on racial grounds. *Hunter v. Erickson*, 393 U.S. 385 (1969) invalidated a city charger amendment adopted by the voters of Akron, Ohio that required any fair housing legislation to be ratified by public referendum, since it selectively imposed heavier electoral burdens on laws favored by groups opposing racial, ethnic and religious discrimination in housing. "[T]he State may no more disadvantage any particular group by making it more difficult to enact legislation in its behalf than it may dilute any person's vote or give any group a smaller representation than another of comparable size." *Washington v. Seattle School District No. 1*, 458 U.S. 457 (1982) relied on *Hunter* to strike down a vote initiative to prohibit

groups"—not just those who are members of traditionally suspect classes, such as racial or ethnic minorities—and any infringement of that right had to pass strict judicial scrutiny.

The mode of constitutional analysis adopted by the Colorado court provides helpful perspective for an examination of Justice Kennedy's opinion in *Romer*. But note, first, that three basic standards have evolved for judicial review of legislation under the Equal Protection Clause: strict scrutiny, as applied by the *Romer* state courts, imposes a burden of justification for legislative action that the government seldom, if ever, is able to meet; a heightened or "intermediate standard" of judicial review that is more tolerant of distinctions or classifications drawn by the legislature or in government regulation; and a deferential "rationality" standard that almost always leads to judicial vindication of the government's defense of class-based distinctions in economic and social legislation. If the statute classifies by a "quasi-suspect" class, such as gender[5] or illegitimacy[6], the intermediate standard of review applies, and the court will uphold the law only if it is substantially related to an important governmental interest. There are two circumstances under which strict scrutiny will apply: the statute classifies by a "suspect" class—such as race, alienage, or national origin[7]—or the statute impinges fundamental rights protected by the Constitution.[8] Laws that are subject to this most "searching" standard of judicial review will be sustained only if they are supported by a "compelling state interest" and are "narrowly tailored" to achieve that interest in the least restrictive manner possible.[9]

The approach of the Colorado Supreme Court extended strict scrutiny to a law classifying persons on the basis of sexual orientation without deciding whether homosexuals, lesbians, or bisexuals constitute a "suspect class." The suspect class contention has met with near universal rejection by the courts since *Bowers v. Hardwick* and was not even an issue on appeal in *Romer*. In effect, however, the fundamental rights analysis permitted the Colorado courts to circumvent that more controversial issue, yet thrust on the state the same

student busing for desegregation purposes because it impermissibly interfered with the political process and unlawfully burdened the efforts of minority groups to secured public benefits.

[5] *Mississippi University for Women v. Hogan*, 458 U.S. 718 (1982); *Craig v. Boren*, 429 U.S. 190 (1976).

[6] *E.G. Trimble v. Gordon*, 430 U.S. 762 (1977).

[7] *Clebrune v. Cleburne Living Center, Inc.*, 473 U.S. 432, 440 (1985).

[8] *E.g. San Antonio School District v. Rodriguez*, 411 U.S. 1 (1973).

weighty burden of justification for Amendment 2, virtually assuring a judicial finding of invalidity. Of course, this approach is inherently limited to legislation that impinges without justification upon rights—procreation,[10]access to the judicial process,[11] interstate travel,[12] and voting[13]—that have been declared "fundamental" by the Supreme Court for constitutional purposes.

Various elements of the Colorado courts' reasoning reverberate in Justice Kennedy's opinion for the *Romer* majority of the U.S. Supreme Court, but with important distinction that may narrow its force as precedent in other factual contexts. Amendment 2's main constitutional defects, for Justice Kennedy, were the "Sweeping and comprehensive" nature of the legal disability it imposed and the fact that it targeted a "solitary class" for legal disenfranchisement, all without "rational" justification. The gist of his analysis was that "Amendment 2 fails, even defies" traditional equal protection analysis because its "impos[es] a broad and undifferentiated disability on a single named group," a disability so sweeping as to be seemingly "inexplicable by anything but animus toward the class that it affects." Notably, however, Justice Kennedy did not explicitly adopt the fundamental rights analysis employed by the state courts nor did the majority formally confer "suspect class" status upon the group or class of individuals disadvantaged by Amendment 2. Instead of "strict scrutiny" applied to defeat the measure below, the *Romer* majority framed its constitutional analysis in terms of traditional "rational basis" equal protection. Rationality review is typically quite lenient: "Unless a statute employs a classification that is inherently invidious or that impinges on fundamental rights,...this Court properly exercises only a limited review power...".[14] At least in theory, it is most deferential to the state, that is, it permits legislative classifications that discriminate for any "reasonable" or "legitimate" governmental purpose.

It may be open to question, however, whether the *Romer* majority, by summarily rejecting Colorado's asserted justifications for Amendment 2, may have implicitly adopted a less deferential approach to state legislative

---

[9] *Adarand Constructors v. Pena*, 115 S. Ct 2097 (1995).

[10] *Shinner v. Oklahoma*, 316 U.S. 535 (1942).

[11] *Douglas v. California*, 372 U.S. 353 (1963).

[12] *Shapiro v. Thompson*. 394 U.S. 618 (1969).

[13] *Kramer v. Union Free School District*, 395 U.S. 621 (1969).

[14] *Schweiker v. Wilson*, 450 U.S. 221, 230 (1981).

classifications than traditional rational basis review. In *Romer*, the withdrawal of legal protection from lesbians and homosexuals was defended by the state as an expression of respect for the associational freedoms other citizens, particularly landlords or employers who have personal or religious objections to homosexuality, and in the interest of conserving resources to combat discrimination against other groups. "Rational basis" equal protection review ordinarily dictates judicial approval of governmental classifications in laws that discriminate on grounds other than race, gender, or ethnicity if any set of circumstances could reasonably or rationally be conceived to support the challenged state action. The Court has even held that burden is on the challenger, not the government, to prevail by discrediting all conceivable justifications. "A State...had no obligation to produce evidence to sustain the rationality of a statutory classification...[T]he burden is on the one attacking the legislative arrangement to negative every conceivable basis which might support it."[15] Nonetheless, the *Romer* majority dismissed the justifications advanced by the State in favor of Amendment 2 with minimal explanation other that its conclusion that "[t]he breadth of the Amendment is so far removed from these particular justifications that we find it impossible to credit them."

The answer may lie in Justice Kennedy's repeated allusions to a possible class-based "animus" by Colorado voters and to the "disadvantage...born of animosity toward the class of persons affected" that may have motivated the popular effort to adopt Amendment 2. This may have provoked the Court to apply an "active" standard of judicial review more rigorous than traditional rationality but less demanding than strict scrutiny. The leading example of such an approach is *Cleburne v. Cleburne Living Center*[16] where the Court invalidated a municipal requirement that homes for the mentally retarded obtain a special permit not required of other care and multiple dwelling facilities. In so doing, the Court rejected the holding of the Court of Appeals that mental retardation was a quasi-suspect classification under the Equal Protection Clause. However, the Court went on to apply an "active" rationality review and struck down the City requirement: "[M]ere negative attitudes, or fear, unsubstantiated by factors which are properly cognizable in a zoning proceeding, are not permissible bases for treating a home for the mentally

---

[15] *Heller v. Doe,* 509 U.S. 312, 319-20 (1993).
[16] 473 U.S. 432 (1985).

retarded differently from apartment buildings, multiple dwellings, and the like."[17] The Court concluded: "[The] short of it is that requiring the permit in this case appears to us to rest on an irrational prejudice against the mentally retarded."[18] An "invigorated" rationality standard is also apparent in certain lower federal court decisions which have called for an affirmative governmental showing of the "rational basis" for traditional military policies toward homosexuals.

Justice Scalia, joined by Justice Thomas and the Chief Justice in dissent, drew largely from *Bowers v. Hardwick,* arguing in effect that state power to criminalize homosexual conduct necessarily entailed authority to impose lesser sanctions "merely disfavoring" such conduct. He also insisted that Amendment 2 had been adopted by the "most democratic procedures" for the "eminently reasonable" purpose of curbing "piecemeal deterioration of the sexual morality favored by a majority of Coloradoans," and chided the majority for promoting the "elitist" judgment that "animosity" toward homosexuality is…evil."

ANALYSIS

The most immediate effect of *Romer,* of course will be felt in other state and local jurisdictions with laws like Amendment 2, adopted by statute, ordinance, or constitutional amendment to bar legal protection for lesbians and homosexuals. A month after *Romer*, for example, the Court granted a petition to review *Equality Foundation for Greater Cincinnati, Inc. v. City of Cincinnati* and promptly remanded for reconsideration by the Sixth Circuit in light of *Romer.*[19] Cincinnati, Ohio voters had enacted a similar measure at the city level one year after the passage of Amendment 2. Issue 3 was a city charger amendment that prohibited the city form enacting any law or policy that gave rise to a claim of discrimination in employment, housing, or public accommodations on the basis of sexual orientation. Gay rights proponents challenged the measure in federal district court and won on a variety of issues, including the right to equal political participation. The Sixth Circuit

---

[17] *Id.* at 448.
[18] *Id.* at 450.
[19] No. 95-239, 64 U.S.L.W. 3122 (S. Ct. 6-17-96).

subsequently reversed and a petition for certiorari was filed.[20] Reportedly, at least eight other states have had campaigns underway for similar state constitutional amendments.[21]

The long range legal implications of *Romer* are more difficult to decipher. The decision has to be read, first, in light of the "exceptional" and "unprecedented" nature of the state law under challenge which, according to Justice Kennedy, amounted to "a general announcement that gays and lesbians shall not have any particular protections from the law." Indeed, it was the "broad and undifferentiated" character of the legal disability imposed, more than any other factor, that convinced the majority of Amendment 2's illegitimate birthright, leading to its invalidation after only a cursory inquiry into rational basis. Accordingly, *Romer* may be a faulty predictor of the outcome in future cases alleging homosexual discrimination over a narrower field—whether marriage, domestic relations and custody matters, military policy or otherwise—where judicial inquiry into legislative rationale may be more meaningful. In particular, the impact of *Romer* on the legal controversy surrounding the rights of gays in the military may still have to be viewed through the prism of the established constitutional principle according "special deference to the military in the conduct of its own affairs."[22]

A second major contributor to the demise of Amendment 2 was the fact that it visited legal disability upon a "single *named* group," identified by a "single trait," and set apart for "disfavored legal status or general hardship." Consequently, had Amendment 2 been framed in neutral terms to negate legal protection for heterosexuals as well as homosexuals on the same generic ground—i.e. substitute "sexual orientation" for "homosexual, lesbian, and bisexual..."—it might possibly have withstood the *Romer* challenge and accomplished its intended objectives. Similarly, while the state may not legally disable a specific group without rational basis, *Romer* did not decide—nor does it necessarily imply—that state legislation that omits certain groups from civil rights coverage or other legal benefits is thereby subject to equal

---

[20] *Equality Foundation v. City of Cincinnati*, 860 F. Supp. 417 (S.D. Ohio), *aff'd in part, vacated in part*, 54 F .3d 261 (1995)., *pet for cert, filed*, No. 95-239) 64 U.S.L.W. 3122 (U.S. 8-10-95).

[21] *See Fight the Right Project, National Gay and Lesbian Task Force Policy Institute, Anti-Gay Initiative Under Consideration I* (1993).

[22] *See* IB96029, "Homosexuals and U.S. Military Policy: Current Issues," at p. 6 (Legal Challenges)(updated June 14, 1996).

protection challenge. No affirmative duty to legislate is necessarily implied by *Romer*. Thirdly, extracted from its specific factual context, the scale of protection afforded by the decision may be limited to traditional rational basis review which, as explained above, is the equal protections standard most tolerant of distinctions drawn between persons and groups in law and governmental policymaking. In other words, the Court's analysis and decision may have been the same if the "single named group" had been lawyers, smokers, or hazardous waste disposers instead of gay rights advocates. Note, however, that due to the lack of elaboration provided by the majority's relatively terse opinion, any conclusions on these and related legal issues are mere speculation until the Courts speaks again.

Nonetheless, by finding that Amendment 2 discriminated against homosexuals, lesbians, and bisexuals as a group—even though not a "suspect" class—*Romer* may have blunted the persuasive force of *Bowers v. Hardwick*. *Bowers*, as noted, had refused to fashion a due process right of privacy to protect persons engaged in homosexual conduct, a holding that had since been widely invoked by federal appellate courts to reject most discrimination claims based on homosexual status as well. "If the Court [in *Bowers]* was unwilling to object to state laws that criminalize the behavior that defines the class, it is hardly open...to conclude that state sponsored discrimination against the class is invidious. After all, there can hardly be more palpable discrimination against a class than making the conduct that defines the class criminal."[23] Indeed, Justice Scalia urged much the same view in his *Romer* dissent, "If it is constitutionally permissible for a State to make homosexual conduct criminal, surely it is possible for a State to enact other laws merely *disfavoring* homosexual conduct."[24] It seems unlikely now that *Bowers* will be viewed to stand for more than it s specific holding—that there is no constitutionally protected liberty interest in homosexual conduct—but even that principle may be less secure given the decision's narrow 5-4 margin and the Court's reconstitution in the past decade.

A final comment on the same sex marriage issue. The Hawaiian state courts are presently considering the constitutional status of that state's policy forbidding same-sex marriage pursuant to an earlier judicial determination that sex is a "suspect classification" for equal protection purposes under the state

---

[23] *Padula v. Webster,* 822 F. 2d 97, 103 (1987).

[24] Opinion of Scalia, J. (dissenting)(slip opinion) at p.7.

constitution. [25] As noted, *Romer* made no explicit suspect class determination—indeed, the issue was not even raised on appeal—and Justice Kennedy employed a rationality standard to evaluate Amendment 2. State prohibitions on same sex marriage, while they carry obvious economic and social consequences, may be distinguishable from the wholesale withdrawal of legal protection for homosexuals and lesbians imposed by Colorado. First, by defining marriage as the union of a man and woman, it may be more difficult to argue that these laws impose a "special disability" on a "named group" since they are neutral on their face and apply to all persons regardless of sexual orientation. Moreover, in *Bowers v. Hardwick*, the Court denied homosexual conduct shelter within the zone of constitutional privacy primarily by reason of historical and constitutional tradition. All thirteen original states had anti-sodomy laws when the Bill of Rights was ratified, and contemporary laws remained in most states, so that "to claim that a right to engage in such conduct is...'deeply rooted in this Nation's history and tradition' or 'implicit in the concept of ordered liberty' is, at best, facetious."[26] The Court also explicitly denied any constitutional "connection between family, marriage, or procreation" and "homosexual activity." Arguably, cultural history and tradition may likewise be factors relevant to judicial evaluation of the same-sex marriage rights after *Romer*, at least until *Bowers* is explicitly overruled.

[25] See *Baehr v. Lewin*, 852 P .2d 44 (Haw. 1993).
[26] 478 U.S. at 194.

SEXUAL ORIENTATION DISCRIMINATION IN EMPLOYMENT

Mark Eddy

BACKGROUND

A federal bill prohibit discrimination nationwide on the basis of sexual orientation was first introduced by Representative Abzug, with four original co-sponsors, in the 94th Congress in 1975, That bill, H.R. 166, would have amended the Civil Rights Act of 1964, as amended,[1] and the Fair Housing Act of 1968, as amended,[2] to prohibit discrimination on the basis of "affectional or sexual preference" in the areas of employment, housing, public accommodations and facilities, public education, and federally assisted programs. Similar bills have been introduced in the House in each succeeding Congress, and in the Senate beginning with S. 1432 in the 99th Congress in 1985 and ending with S. 574 in the 102nd Congress in 1991. (Bills to prohibit discrimination on the basis of sexual orientation *only in employment* were introduced in the Senate in the 96th through 98th Congresses.) Except for

---

[1] 42 U.S.C. 2000a *et seq.*
[2] 42 U.S.C. 3601 *et.seq.*

hearings held in 1980[3] and 1982,[4] these bills to amend the Civil Rights Act have not seen action in any Congress.

The 103rd Congress marked a departure from this historical pattern of introducing "gay rights bills" that would amend the Civil Rights and Fair Housing Acts. Although the traditional bill covering employment, housing, and other forms of discrimination was introduced in the House early in the first session of the 103rd Congress (H.R. 423/Towns), it was not introduced in the Senate. Congressional supporters of gay rights legislation, decided to drop the more broadly based approach of earlier Congresses in favor of the Employment Non-Discrimination Act (ENDA), which would affect only the area of employment and would create new law instead of amending the Civil Rights Act. Accordingly, on June 23, 1994, H.R. 4636 was introduced by Representative Studds with 108 co-sponsors, and S. 2238 was introduced by Senator Kennedy with 29 co-sponsors.

Except for hearings held on July 29, 1994, by the Senate Committee on Labor and Human Resources,[5] there were no further actions on either bill.

On June 15, 1995, ENDA was reintroduced in both houses of the 104th Congress. H. R. 1863 was introduced by Representative Studds with 118 co-sponsors, and S. 932 was introduced by Senator Jeffords with 20 co-sponsors. The House bill was referred principally to the Committee on Economic and Educational Opportunities. (The Government Programs Subcommittee of the House Small Business Committee held oversight hearings on the measure on July 17, 1996.)[6] The Senate bill was referred to the Committee on Labor and Human Resources. Similarly worded except for a "Purposes" section included in the Senate version, the bills contained the same provisions.

---

[3] U.S. Congress, House Committee on Education and Labor, Subcommittee on Employment Opportunities, *Civil Rights Amendments Act of 1979,*hearing on H.R. 2074, 96th Cong., 2nd sess., Oct 10, 1980 (Washington: GPO, 1980).

[4] U.S. Congress, House Committee on Education and Labor, Subcommittee on Employment Opportunities, *Hearing on Civil Rights Act Amendments of 1981*, hearing on H.R. 1454, 97th Cong., 2nd sess., Jan. 27, 1982 (Washington: GPO, 1982).

[5] U.S. Congress, Senate Committee on Labor and Human Resources, *Employment Non-Discrimination Act of 1994,* hearing on S. 2238, 103rd Cong., 2nd sess., July 16, 1996 (Washington: GPO, 1996).

[6] U.S. Congress, House Committee on Small Business, Subcommittee on Government Programs, *The Employment Non-Discrimination Act*, hearing on H.R. 1863, 104th Cong., 2nd sess., July 16, 1996 (Washington: GPO, 1996).

President Clinton first announced his support for ENDA on October 19, 1995, in a letter to Senator Kennedy. He has reiterated his support on subsequent occasions, most notably, perhaps, in his 1999 State of the Union address.[7]

In September 1996, during the Senate's consideration of the Defense of Marriage Sct (H.R. 3396/Barr),[8] there was an attempt to attach ENDA to the Defense of Marriage Act as an amendment. Consequently, EDNA was debated on the Senate floor on September 6 and 10, 1996.[9] At the close of debate, the measure failed to pass by a vote of 49-50. (This marked the first and only floor vote in any Congress to prohibit discrimination on the basis of sexual orientation in a nonmilitary setting). The version of ENDA actually considered was S. 2056, introduced by Senator Kennedy on September 5, 1996. Similar to S. 932, it contained a new section stating: "Nothing in this Act shall be construed to prohibit a covered entity from enforcing rules regarding non-private sexual conduct, if such rules of conduct are designed for, and uniformly applied to, all individuals regardless of sexual orientation."

A rewritten version of ENDA that included this new section was reintroduced in the 105th Congress on June 10, 1997. S. 869 was introduced by Senator Jeffords with 34 co-sponsors, and H.R. 1858 was introduced by Representative Shays with 149 co-sponsors. The Senate bill was referred to the Committee on Labor and Human Resources, which held a hearing on October 23, 1997.[10] The identical House bill was referred principally to the Committee on Education and the Workforce, and in addition to the Committees on House Oversight, Government Reform and Oversight, and the Judiciary. Neither bill saw any further action in either chamber.

---

[7] U.S. President (Clinton), "Address Before a Joint Session of the Congress on the State of the Union," *Weekly Compilation of Presidential Document,* vol. 35, Jan. 19, 1999, p. 87. Also at http://www.pub.whitehouse.gov/uri-res/I2R?urn:pdi//oma.eop.gov.us/1999/1/20/1.text.1

[8] For background and pro-con analysis of the Defense of Marriage Act (P.L. 104-109), see: U.S. Library of Congress, Congressional Research Service, *Defense of Marriage Act,* by Mark Eddy, CRS Report 96-589 GOV (Washington: Dec 4, 1996).

[9] "Employment Nondiscrimination Act of 1996," *Congressional Record*, daily edition, vol. 142, Sept 6, 1996, pp. S9986-10005, and Sept, 10, 1996, pp. S10129-10139.

[10] U.S. Congress, Senate Committee on Labor and Human Resources, *Employment Non-Discrimination Act of 1997, hearings on S. 869, 105th Cong., 1st sess., Oct. 23, 1997 (Washington: GPO, 1998).*

ENDA IN THE 106TH CONGRESS

Rewritten to more closely parallel the unlawful employment practice revisions of Title VII of the Civil Rights Act of 1964, as amended,[11] and to more specifically prohibit affirmative action as a remedy for violations of the proposed act, ENDA was reintroduced in the 106th Congress on June 24, 1999. The Senate version (S. 1276) was introduced by Senators Jeffords, Kennedy, and Lieberman, with 32 additional co-sponsors. IT was referred t the Committee on Health, Education, Labor, and Pensions. The identically-worded House bill (H.R. 2355) was introduced by Representatives Shays and Frank with 14 additional co-sponsors. It was referred principally to the Committee on Education and the Workforce, and in addition to the Committees on House Administration, Government Reform, and the Judiciary for consideration of such provisions as fall within the jurisdictions of the respective committees.

The bills would make it illegal for both public and private employers and for labor unions to discriminate against individuals on the basis of sexual orientation with respect to hiring and firing decisions, compensation, and terms, conditions, or privileges of employment. Nor could employers or labor unions limit, segregate, or classify individuals in any way, on the basis of sexual orientation, that would deprive or tend to deprive them of employment opportunities. Discrimination against any person due to sexual orientation would also be prohibited in training, retraining, apprenticeship, and on-the-job training programs.

Employment agencies, joint labor-management committees, Senate and House employers, and congressional agencies would also be covered. As is the case with the Civil Rights Act of 1964, employers with fewer than 15 employees and labor unions with fewer than 15 members would be excluded from coverage. ENDA would take effect 60 days after its enactment and would not apply to conduct that occurred before the effective date. It would cover paid workers only and not uncompensated volunteers.

The proposed act would not apply to the U.S. armed forces, to *bona fide* private membership clubs, or to religious organizations. The bills provide that the religious exemption would include colleges, schools, or universities that are run by religious organizations or that promote a particular religion. A

---

[11] 42 U.S.C. 2000e *et seq.*

religious organization's for profit activities that are subject to taxation, however, would be covered. The bills as introduced would specifically prohibit employment quotas and preferential treatment based on sexual orientation. Also prohibited would be the use of statistical evidence to support a finding of discrimination on the basis of sexual orientation (as can be done in cases involving race or sex) as well as the use of numerical ratios, targets, or other affirmative action quotas as remedies for alleged discrimination on the basis of sexual orientation. The bills specifically state that employers would not be required to provide employee benefits to unmarried domestic partners. (EDNA would not affect marriage, adoption, or child custody laws, all of which are determined by the individual states).

EDNA's enforcement powers would be patterned after those of Title VII of the Civil Rights Act of 1964, as amended. ENDA would be enforced by the Equal Employment Opportunities Commission (EEOC), which would e authorized to issue implementing regulations. (In enforcing equal employment opportunity in the private sector under Title VII, the EEOC is mandated to receive complaints of discrimination and to issue charges of patterns or practices of discrimination without receipt of a complaint.

It investigates complaints and, if it finds reason to believe that a charge is true, seeks to eliminate such discrimination through conciliation. If conciliation fails, the EEOC may file a civil action in a federal district court. The EEOC follows the same enforcement procedures in resolving complaints against state and local governments, except that the Department of Justice must institute any court actions against such respondents. With respect to federal employment, the EEOC is mandated to review appeals from department or agency decisions on complaints of discrimination. In the case of the U.S. Congress, enforcement of the act for congressional employees would be carried out by the Office of Compliance created by the Congressional Accountability Act of 1995.[12])

EDNA would specifically prohibit retaliation or discrimination against a person because that person opposes any action or practice prohibited by the act or because that person makes a charge or participates in an investigation, proceeding, or hearing conducted according to the provisions of the act. Also, ENDA would prohibit coercion, intimidation, threats, or interference with any

---

[12] P.L. 104-1, 109 Stat. 24, 2 U.S.C. 1301 *et seq.*

person who exercises the rights, or encourages others to exercise the rights, granted under the act.

The bills define "sexual orientation" to mean "homosexuality, bisexuality, or heterosexuality, whether the orientation is real or perceived." If enacted, the provisions of ENDA would therefore apply to heterosexuals and bisexuals as well as to gay men and lesbians. Not just homosexuals but everyone would be protected from employment discrimination on the basis of sexual orientation. Men and women who are of heterosexual orientation, for example, but who are perceived on the basis of appearance or behavior to fit a homosexual stereotype, would be protected from job discrimination based on such perceptions. Heterosexuals would also be protected from discrimination by homosexual or bisexual employers.

SEXUAL ORIENTATION DISCRIMINATION IN EMPLOYMENT: PRO-CON ANALYSIS OF ENDA

Mark Eddy

BACKGROUND

The first federal bill that would have prohibited discrimination nationwide on the basis of sexual orientation was introduced by Representative Abzug in the 94th Congress in 1975. Similar bills to prohibit such discrimination in employment, housing, public accommodations, public education, and federally assisted programs have been introduced in each subsequent Congress.

First, introduced in the 103red Congress in June 1994, the Employment Nondiscrimination Act (ENDA) would apply only to the area of employment, both public and private. Its prohibition of discrimination on the basis of sexual orientation would not apply to religious organizations, religious schools, the armed services, or firms with fewer than 15 employees.[1] Reintroduced in the 104th Congress, the bill was considered by the full Senate in September 1996,

---

[1] For a more complete discussion of the provisions of ENDA and of the history of its predecessor bills in Congress, see: U.S. Library of Congress, Congressional Research Service, *Sexual Orientation Discrimination in Employment: Legislation in the 106th Congress,* by Mark Eddy, CRS Report 980587 GOV.

when it failed to pass by a vote of 49-50.[2] ENDA was reintroduced in the 105th Congress in June 1997, and again in the 106th Congress in June 1999 by Senators Jeffords, Kennedy, and Lieberman (S. 1276) and Representatives Shays and Frank (H.R. 2355).

The bills define "sexual orientation" to mean "homosexuality, bisexuality, or heterosexuality, whether the orientation is real or perceived." If enacted, ENDA would therefore apply to heterosexuals as well as to homosexuals and bisexuals. Men and women who are of heterosexual orientation, for example, but who are perceived on the basis of appearance or behavior to fit a homosexual stereotype, would be protected form job discrimination based on such false perceptions. Heterosexuals would also be protected from discrimination by homosexual or bisexual employers.

ENDA's principal impact and major controversy, however, arise from its extension of civil rights protections in employment to homosexuals and bisexuals. The pro-con analysis that follows, therefore, focuses on these groups and ignores the act's application to heterosexuals. (For brevity, the term *homosexual* is used below to refer to both gay men and lesbians and to bisexuals of either sex.).

ARGUMENTS FOR AND AGAINST ENDA

(1)Constitutional Arguments

Opponents of civil rights protections on the basis of sexual orientation argue that the proposed bills violate the "establishment of religion" and "free exercise of religion" clauses of the First Amendment. According to this view, for the government to forbid those whose religion teaches that homosexuality is wrong from discriminating against homosexuals on the basis of that belief would infringe on their free exercise of religion and would violate the separation of church and state. Opponents also cite the 1986 Supreme Court decision in *Bowers v. Hardwick,*[3] which upheld the Georgia sodomy statute, as

[2] "Employment Nondiscrimination Act of 1996," *Congressional Record,* daily edition, vol. 142, Sept 6, 1996, pp. S9986-10005, and Sept. 10, 1996, pp. S10129-10139.
[3] 478 U.S. 186, 106 S. Ct. 2841 (1986).

evidence that homosexual acts, and therefore homosexuals, are not constitutionally protected.

Proponents of the legislation argue that discrimination against homosexuals constitutes a violation of basic rights that are guaranteed to all Americans under the Constitution. They base this reasoning on the due process clauses of the Fifth and Fourteenth Amendments, the equal protection clause of the Fourteenth Amendments, and the implied right to privacy found in the Fourth and Fifth Amendments. Due process rights, for example, are said to be violated by the dismissal of a public school teacher on the grounds of homosexuality. It has also been argued that discrimination against homosexuals by governmental entities violates the First Amendment's separation of church and state insofar as Biblical injunctions are responsible for shaping the belief that homosexual behavior is immoral. In any case, proponents point out, religious organizations are excluded from coverage by the proposed act.

(2)The Nature of Protected Classes

Many opponents of ENDA argue that homosexuals as a class are not deserving of civil rights protection because, unlike the other classes that are already protected by civil rights legislation, the characteristic by which homosexuals are identified is volitional, not innate. Membership in sex, racial, and ethnic classes is a matter of birth, not choice. Homosexuality, however, is said by opponents to be a matter of choice—an immoral, socially repugnant, and in some places illegal choice that should not be protected by law. Homosexuals, in this view, are not comparable to the other protected classes. Instead, they are persons who choose to engage in deviant behavior that is unacceptable to society and is by its very nature beyond the scope of civil rights legislation.

Many proponents argue that one's sexual orientation is not, in fact, a matter of choice any more than is one's sex or race. In this view, homosexuals are comparable to other protected classes, such as women and ethnic and racial minorities, insofar as the characteristic that sets them apart is not chosen but is innate. Therefore, they say, discrimination on the basis of sexual orientation is just as wrong as discrimination on the basis of sex, race, or nationality. Some proponents point out that sexual orientation is sometimes a matter of choice. Some lesbian activists, for example, have stated that they have chosen their sexual orientation on moral or spiritual grounds, making their preferred sexual orientation similar to a religious preference, which is a matter of moral choice that is already protected by civil rights laws.

(3)The Extent of Anti-Homosexual Discrimination

Opponent of extending civil rights protection to homosexuals sometimes argue that the legislation is unnecessary because employment discrimination against homosexuals is not widespread. It would be difficult, they say, to make a case that homosexuals as a class are broadly discriminated against in employment. This view holds that homosexuals, buy their own admission, are present in every profession and that they already enjoy widespread tolerance, especially if they are discreet and do not openly display their sexual orientation. The real objective of homosexual rights activists, according to their opponents, is not access to jobs but the acceptance of homosexuality as a morally legitimate and socially worthy lifestyle under color of federal law.

On the contrary, argue proponents of the proposed legislation, homosexuals in the United States constitute a historically persecuted group. Disclosure of one's homosexuality or even the suspicion of homosexuality frequently results in loss of employment, they say, and actual cases in numerous occupations and jurisdictions can be cited to support the argument that discrimination against homosexuals is widespread and materially injurious. Proponents also argue that passage of ENDA would not condone homosexuality any more than the inclusion of religion in civil rights legislation indicates support for a particular religion or for religion in general. They hold that the passage of ENDA would not and could not touch privately held beliefs that homosexuality is a sin.

(4)Employment Issues

Opponents of ENDA argue that sexual orientation must continue to be considered an employment-qualifying factor, especially in certain occupations. Of particular concern are teachers, pastors, camp counselors, and social workers who deal with children. To permit homosexuals to occupy these nurturing and role-model positions, they assert, could be expected to influence children toward homosexuality.

Opponents also say that passage of the proposed legislation would lead to affirmative-action employment quotas for homosexuals. Although the bills specifically forbid the EEOC from collecting employment data on sexual orientation, forbid the use of statistics to determine that discrimination exists, and forbid the use of numerical quotas in remedying past discrimination, opponents argue that ENDA would be an obvious stepping stone to affirmative action or a quota system in every occupation, as a remedy for perceived past discrimination against homosexuals.

Proponents argue that skills and job performance, not sexual orientation, should determine whether employees are hired, promoted, or fired. Improper behavior or poor performance on the job by homosexuals should be handled in the same way as for heterosexuals. Homosexuals, they say, do not seek special legal protection, such as employment quotas. Rather, they seek equal treatment in the workplace, without regard to sexual orientation, as has already been granted by many corporations that have extended their formal nondiscrimination policies to include gays and lesbians.

Proponents also argue that there is no evidence that homosexuals in role-model positions influence children toward homosexuality. They maintain that in the 10 states and more than 130 local jurisdictions that already protect homosexuals from employment discrimination, no such problems have arisen.

(5)Effects Upon Society

Opponents argue that making discrimination on the basis of sexual orientation illegal would place homosexuality on a par with heterosexuality, thereby undermining heterosexuality, one of the most important cohesive forces in our society. This argument contends that homosexuality would become more widespread and would constitute a direct assault upon the family, thereby diminishing society's procreative powers. Some believe that extending civil rights protections to homosexuals would open the way to acceptance of a wide range of sexual practices now as clearly condemned as sodomy has been, such as group marriage, incest, pedophilia, and bestiality. The passage of ENDA, they believe, would place at risk the moral basis of society as we know it.

Proponents argue that discrimination against homosexuals is harmful because it deprives society of the energies and talents that homosexuals must expend in hiding their sexual orientation. Supposedly, if civil rights protections were granted to homosexuals, these diverted energies and talents would be redirected into productive activities. In this view, the general welfare is diminished when any group is denied full participation in the economic and social life of the nation. This is no less true for homosexuals, it is argued, than for women, blacks, and other groups that are now protected by civil rights laws. Passage of the proposed legislation would benefit not just homosexuals but the society as a whole.

(6) Public Health Issues

Opponents of civil rights protections for homosexuals argue that such laws would increase the exposure of the general public to AIDS, a deadly viral disease that has had its initial and principal impact on the homosexual community in the United States. The public, in this view, has a right to a workplace and marketplace in which the risk of exposure to the AIDS virus is held to a minimum. The danger of exposure to other infectious diseases, such as hepatitis, has also been mentioned by some as a reason for opposing gay rights legislation.

Proponents of the legislation argue that AIDS and other infectious diseases are not homosexual diseases but are human diseases that can affect anyone. They contend that there is no danger of contracting AIDS through casual contact such as occurs in the workplace and in the marketplace, and they point out that the Americans with Disabilities Act[4] already protects persons with HIV infection and AIDS from discrimination in employment, housing, public accommodations, and other areas of life. They argue that no public health danger would arise from extending similar protections to all homosexuals. Furthermore, they say, the employment discrimination that can result from the AIDS epidemic makes ENDA more necessary than ever.

---

[4] P.L. 101-336, 42 U.S.C. 12101 *et seq.*

SEX DISCRIMINATION AND THE UNITED STATES SUPREME COURT: RECENT DEVELOPMENTS IN THE LAW

Karen J. Lewis and Jon O. Shimabukuro

With its recent sex discrimination decisions, the United States Supreme Court has not only further defined the applicability of the equal protection guarantees of the Constitution and the nondiscriminatory polices of federal statutes, but has rejected the use of gender stereotypes and continued to recognize the discriminatory effect of gender hostility in the workplace and in the schools. This report focuses on recent sex discrimination challenges based on the equal protection guarantees of the Fourteenth and Fifth Amendments, Title VII of the Civil Rights Act of 1964, and Title IX of the Education Amendments of 1972. Although the Court's analysis of sex discrimination challenges under the Constitution differs form its analysis of sex discrimination under the two federal statutes discussed in this report, it is apparent that the Court is willing to refine its standards of review under both schemes to accommodate the novel claims presented by these cases.

EQUAL PROTECTION CASES

Constitutional challenges that allege discrimination on the basis of sex are premised either on the equal protection guarantees of the Fourteenth

Amendment or the equal protection component of the Fifth Amendment. To maintain an equal protection challenge, government action must be established, that is, it must be shown that the government, and not a private actor, has acted in a discriminatory manner. While the Fourteenth Amendment prohibits discriminatory conduct by the states, the Fifth Amendment forbids such action by the federal government.

The Fourteenth Amendment provides, in relevant part:

> No state shall make or enforce any law which shall abridge the privileges or immunities of the citizens of the United States; nor shall any State deprive any person of life, liberty, or property, without due process of law; *nor deny to any person within its jurisdiction the equal protection of the laws.*

U.S. CONST. Amen. XIV *(emphasis added.)*

Although the Fourteenth Amendment requires equal protection, it does not preclude the classification of individuals. The Court has noted that the Constitution does not require things which are "different in fact or opinion to be treated in laws as though they were the same."[1] A classification will not offend the Constitution unless it is characterized by invidious discrimination.[2] The Court has adopted three levels of review to establish the presence of invidious discrimination:

Strict scrutiny: This most active form of judicial review has been applied where there is either a suspect classification (*e.g.* race, national origin, alienage) or a burdening of a fundamental interest (*e.g.* privacy, marriage). A classification will survive strict scrutiny if the government can show that it is *necessary* to achieving a *compelling* interest.[3] Most statutory classifications subject to strict scrutiny are invalidated.

Intermediate scrutiny: This level of review is not as rigorous as strict scrutiny. A classification will survive intermediate scrutiny if it is

---

[1] *Tigner v. Texas*, 310 U.S. 141, 147 (1940).

[2] See *Ferguson v. Skrupa*, 372 U.S. 726, 732 (1963).

[3] See *San Antonio Independent School District v. Rodriguez, 411 U.S. (1973).*

substantially related to achieving an *important* government objective.[4] Sex classifications are subject to intermediate scrutiny.

Rational basis review: This least active form of judicial review allows a classification to survive an equal protection challenge if the classification is *rationally related* to a *legitimate* government interest.[5] This level of review is characterized by its deference to legislative judgment. Most economic regulations are subject to rational basis review.

The Court's adoption of intermediate scrutiny for sex classifications did not occur until 1976. In *Craig v. Boren*, the Court declared unconstitutional an Oklahoma statute that prohibited the sale of "non-intoxicating" 3.2% beer to males under the age of 21 and to females under the age of 18.[6] Females above the age of 18, but below 21, were allowed to purchase this beer. Although the Court agreed with the state's argument that the protection of public health and safety is an important government interest, it found that the gender classification employed by the statute was not substantially related to achieving that goal. The statistical evidence presented by the state to show that more 18 to 20-year-old males were arrested for drunk driving and that males between the ages of 17 and 21 were over represented among those injured in traffic accidents could not establish that the statute's gender classification was substantially related to ensuring public health and safety.[7] In addition to their methodological problems, the statistics failed to establish the dangerousness of non-intoxicating 3.2% beer for purposes of distinguishing between males and females.

In establishing an intermediate level of review for sex classifications, the *Craig* Court identified what has been a common theme in sex discrimination cases under the Fourteenth Amendment: stereotypes and generalizations about

---

[4] See *Craig v. Boren*, 429 U.S. 190, 197 (1976).

[5] See *Lindsley v. National Carbonic Gas CO.*, 220 U.S. 61 (1911); *Royster Guano Co. v. Virginia*, 253 U.S. 412 (1920); *San Antonio School District v. Rodriguez*, 411 U.S. 1 (1973); *Mass Bd. Of Retirement v. Murgia*, 427 U.S. 307 (1976); *Maher v. Roe*, 432 U.S. 464 (1977).

[6] 429 U.S. 190 (1976).

[7] The state also introduced the following: a random roadside survey that indicated that young males were more inclined to drive and drink and drink beer than were their female equivalents. FBI nationwide statistics showing an increase in arrests for drunk driving; and similar statistics from other jurisdictions.

the sexes.[8] In *Craig*, the Court acknowledged its previous invalidation of statutes that premised their classifications on misconceptions concerning the role of females. The Court's rejection of the use of stereotypes may be seen in many of the cases in this area.[9] The Court's most recent decisions allude similarly to the use of stereotypes and generalizations.

In *J.E.B. v. Alabama*, the Court determined that the state could not use its peremptory challenges to exclude male jurors in a paternity and child support action.[10] In reaching its conclusion, the Court reviewed the historical exclusion of women form juries because of the belief that women were "too fragile and virginal to withstand the polluted courtroom atmosphere."[11] In *J.E.B.*, the Court questioned the state's generalizations of male jurors being more sympathetic to the arguments of a father in a paternity action and female jurors being more receptive to the mother. The Court maintained that state actors who exercise peremptory challenges in reliance on gender stereotypes "ratify and reinforce prejudicial views of the relative abilities of men and women."[12] The Court feared that this discriminatory use of peremptory challenges would not only raise questions about the fairness of the entire proceedings, but also create the impression of the judicial system acquiescing in the denial of participation by one gender.

In *U.S. v. Virginia*, the Court conducted a more searching form of intermediate scrutiny to find unconstitutional the exclusion of women from the Virginia Military Institute (VMI).[13] While articulating the need to show that a classification is substantially related to an important government interest, the Court also required the state to establish an "exceedingly persuasive justification" for its actions.[14]

---

[8] 429 U.S. at 198.

[9] See *Califano v. Goldfarb*, 420 U.S. 199 (1977) (Invalidated section of the Social Security Act that permitted survivors' benefits for male widows only if they were receiving half of their support from their wives); *Orr v. Orr*, 440 U.S. 268 (1979) (Invalidated Alabama statute that imposed alimony obligations on husbands, but not wives); *Caban v. Mohammed*, 441 U.S. 380 (1979) (Invalidated New York statute that required the consent of the mother, but not the father, to permit the adoption of an illegitimate child); *Mississippi University for Women v. Hogan*, 458 U.S. 718 (1982) (Invalidated policy of a state-supported university that limited admission to its nursing school to women on the grounds that it reinforced traditional stereotypes.).

[10] 511 U.S. 127 (1994).

[11] 511 U.S. at 133.

[12] 511 U.S. at 141.

[13] 518 U.S. 515 (1996).

[14] *Id.*

Virginia advanced two arguments in support of VMI's exclusion of women: first, the single-sex education offered by VMI contributed to a diversity of educational approaches in Virginia; second, VMI employed a unique adversative method of training that would be destroyed if women were admitted.[15]

After reviewing the history of Virginia's educational system, the Court concluded that VMI was not established or maintained to promote educational diversity. In fact, VMI's "historic and constant plan" was to offer a unique educational benefit to only men.[16] VMI was not meant to complement other Virginia institutions as a single-sex educational option. Further, the Court recognized Virginia's historic reluctance to allow women to pursue higher education. Any interest Virginia had in maintaining educational diversity seemed to be "proffered in response to litigation."[17]

In addressing Virginia's second argument, the Court expressed concern over the exclusion of women from VMI because of generalizations about their ability. While acknowledging that most women would probably not choose the adversative method, the Court maintained that some women had the will and capacity to succeed at VMI. Following *J.E.B.*, the Court cautioned state actors to not rely on overbroad generalizations to perpetuate patterns of discrimination. While the Court believed that the adversative method did promote important goals, it concluded that the exclusion of women was not substantially related to achieving those goals.

After determining that VMI's exclusion of women violated the Fourteenth Amendment, the Court reviewed the state's remedy, a separate program for women. Virginia established the Virginia Women's Institute for Leadership (VWIL) following the adverse decision of he court of appeals. Unlike VMI, VWIL did not use the adversative method because it was believed to be inappropriate for most women.[18] VWIL lacked the faculty, facilities, and course offerings available at VMI. Because VWIL was not a comparable single-sex institution for women, the Court concluded that it was an inadequate remedy for the state's equal protection violations. VMI subsequently became coeducational.

---

[15] See also Kimberly D. Jones, *United States v. Virginia: The Constitutionality of Public Single-Sex Schools*, CRS Report 96-924 A.

[16] 518 U.S. at 540.

[17] 518 U.S. at 533.

[18] 518 U.S. at 549.

The Court addressed gender stereotypes in a third case involving immigration issues. In *Miller v. Albright,* the Court considered a challenge to § 309 of the Immigration and Nationality Act.[19] The petitioner, the child of an American father and a Filipino mother, contended that § 309 imposed additional requirements for establishing American citizenship when a child is fathered by an American citizen outside of the United States.[20] For children born of a citizen mother and an alien father, citizenship is established at birth. However, for children born of a citizen father and an alien mother, citizenship is not established until the father or the child takes affirmative steps to confirm their relationship by the child's eighteenth birthday. In this case, the petitioner's father did not attempt to establish his relationship with his daughter until after her eighteenth birthday. Thus, the petitioner's application for citizenship was denied.

The case produced five different opinions. While six justices agreed that the petitioner's complaint should be dismissed, they provided different reasons for this conclusion. Justices Stevens and Rehnquist maintained that § 309's distinction between "illegitimate" children of U.S. citizen mothers and "illegitimate" children of U.S. citizen fathers is permissible because it is "eminently reasonable and justified by important Government policies.[21] Justices O'Connor and Kennedy contended, however, that the distinction could withstand only rational basis review and should not satisfy the kind of heightened scrutiny Justice Stevens seemed to conduct. Setting aside the issue of § 309's constitutionality, Justices O'Connor and Kennedy believed that the petitioner lacked the standing necessary to even pursue her claim. Finally, Justices Scalia and Thomas contended that the petitioner's complaint should be dismissed because the Court lacks the power to confer citizenship. Having acknowledged that Congress has the exclusive authority to grant citizenship, Justices Scalia and Thomas believed that there was no need to address the constitutionality of § 309. Justices Ginsberg, Breyer, and Souter dissented in opinions written by Justices Ginsberg and Breyer.

In their separate opinions, Justices Stevens, O'Connor, Ginsburg, and Breyer each addressed the petitioner's argument that § 309 invokes gender stereotypes. The petitioner contended that § 309 relies on the belief that an

[19] 523 U.S. 420, 118 S.Ct 1428 (1998).

[20] See 8 U.S.C. § 1409.

[21] 118 S.Ct. at 1440.

American father "remains aloof from day-to-day child rearing duties," and will not be as close to his child.[22]

Justice Stevens maintained that the statue has a non-stereotypical purpose of ensuring the existence of a blood relationship between father and child. Justice Stevens recognized that the distinction is reasonable because mothers have the opportunity to establish parentage at birth, while fathers do not always have that opportunity. Further, he contended that the distinction encourages the development of a healthy relationship between the citizen and the foreign-born child, and fosters ties between the child and the United States. Thus, § 309's additional requirements are appropriate for fathers, but unnecessary for mothers.

In their dissenting opinions, Justices Ginsburg and Breyer contended that § 309 relies on generalizations about men and women and the ties they maintain with their children. Justice Ginsberg argued that § 309's goals of assuring ties between the citizen father and the foreign-born child, and between the child and the United States can be achieved without reference to gender. Justice Breyer argued similarly, positing a distinction between caretaker and non-caretaker parents, rather than mother and father.

While the Court's recent decisions involving sex and equal protection illustrate that is concerned with the stereotyping of men and women, it is unclear whether it will continue to subject sex classifications and any related stereotypes to a traditional form of intermediate scrutiny. The Court's requirement of an "exceedingly persuasive justification" in *VMI* suggests that it may be interested in conducting a more exacting form of judicial review for sex classifications. In his *Miller* dissent, Justice Breyer emphasized the need to apply the standard established in *VMI.* Should the Court move definitively toward a higher level of judicial review, it is possible that sex may be considered a suspect classification like race, national origin, or alienage. However, even if that does not occur, the Court's decision in *VMI* suggests that equal protection analysis may be moving toward only two levels of review: heightened scrutiny and rational basis review.

---

[22] 118 S.Ct. at 1441.

TITLE VII OF THE CIVIL RIGHTS ACT OF 1964

Title VII prohibits an employer from discriminating against any individual with respect to hiring or the terms and condition of employment because of such individual's race, color, religion, sex, or national origin.[23] Sex discrimination cases under Title VII have involved sexual harassment, pregnancy discrimination, and wage disparities among employees.[24]

The Court has developed two principal models for proving claims of employment discrimination.[25] The "disparate treatment" model focuses on an employer's intent to discriminate. Alternately, the "disparate impact" model is concerned with the adverse effects of an employer's practices on a protected class. Disparate impact analysis may find a facially neutral employment practice to be violative of Title VII even without evidence of the employer's subjective intent to discriminate. To succeed, a plaintiff must demonstrate that the application of a specific employment practiced has had a disparate impact on a particular group of employees.[26]

Both disparate treatment and disparate impact analysis involve a system of evidentiary burden shifting. Both models require the plaintiff to establish a prima facie case of discrimination. If such a case can be established, the burden shifts to the employer to articulate a defense for its actions. At that

---

[23] Title VII provides, in relevant part, that it is an unlawful employment practice for an employer

(1) to fail or refuse to hire or to discharge any individual, or otherwise to discriminate against
any individual with respect to his compensation, terms, conditions, or privileges of employment, because of such individual's race, color, religion, sex or national origin; or

(2) to limit, segregate, or classify his employees or applicants for employment in any way
which would deprive or tend to deprive any individual of employment opportunities or otherwise adversely affect his status as an employee, because of such individual's race, color, religion, sex, or national origin.

42 U.S.C. § 2000e-2.

[24] See also Karen J. Lewis, *Sex Discrimination and the United States Supreme Court Developments in the Law*, CRS Report 89-500A.

[25] See also Charles V. Dale, *The Civil Rights Act of 1991: A Legal Analysis of Various Proposals to Reform the Federal Equal Employment Opportunity Laws,* CRS Report 91-757A.

[26] See also *Ward's Cove Packing Company v. Atonio*, 490 U.S. 642 (1989).

point, the employer may produce evidence showing that its actions are justified because of the needs of its business. Alternately, the employer may contend that otherwise discriminatory conduct satisfies a bona fide occupational qualification (BFOQ). Under § 703(e)(1) of Title VII, an employer may discriminate on the basis of "religion, sex, or national origin is a bona fide occupational qualification reasonably necessary to the normal operation of that particular business or enterprise."[27] Ultimately, however, the plaintiff retains the burden of persuasion; that is, the plaintiff must disprove the employer's assertion that the adverse employment action or practice is based on business necessity or is a BFOQ.

PREGNANCY DISCRIMINATION

In recent years, the Court has addressed Title VII and sex discrimination most frequently in the context of sexual harassment. In *UAW v. Johnson Controls,* however, the Court considered whether an employer may discriminate against fertile women because of its interest in protecting potential fetuses.[28]

Johnson Controls, a battery manufacturer, implemented a policy that excluded "women who are pregnant or who are capable of bearing children" from jobs that exposed them to lead.[29] Lead was the primary ingredient in the manufacturing process at Johnson Controls. Although fertile women were excluded from employment, fertile men were still permitted to work.

The Court found that Johnson Control's policy was facially discriminatory because it did not apply to the reproductive capacity of the company's male employees in the same way it applied to that of female employees. The Court's conclusion was bolstered by the Pregnancy Discrimination Act of 1978 (PDA), which provides that discrimination "on the basis of sex" for purposes of violating Title VII includes discrimination "because of or on the basis or pregnancy, childbirth, or related medical conditions."[30]

---

[27] 42 U.S.C. § 2000e-2(e)(1).

[28] 499 U.S. 187 (1991). See also Gina M. Stevens, *Sex-Based Discrimination: UAW v. Johnson Controls, Inc.*, CRS Report 91-323A.

[29] 499 U.S. at 192.

[30] See 42 U.S.C. § 2000e(k).

Although Johnson Controls asserted that sex was a BFOQ for protecting fetal safety, the Court maintained that discrimination on the bases of sex for safety concerns is allowed only in narrow circumstances.[31] The Court stressed that to qualify as a BFOQ, an employment practice must relate to the essence or central mission of the employer's business.[32] Because the potential fetuses of Johnson Controls' females employees were not customers or third parties whose safety was essential to the business of battery manufacturing, the Court rejected Johnson Controls' BFOQ defense.

SEXUAL HARASSMENT

Courts have recognized two forms of sexual harassment under Title VII. The first, quid, pro quo sexual harassment, occurs when submission to unwelcome sexual advances or other conduct of a sexual nature is made a condition of an individual's employment or is otherwise used as the basis for employment decisions. The second form of harassment involves conduct that has the purpose or effect of interfering unreasonably with an individual's work performance or of creating a hostile or offensive working environment. This second form of sexual harassment is referred to as "hostile environment" sexual harassment.

In *Harris v. Forklift Systems, Inc.*, the Court sought to define when a workplace was sufficiently "hostile" for purposes of maintaining a claim under Title VII.[33] The petitioner, a female manager at an equipment rental company, alleged that the company's president created a hostile environment by repeatedly insulting her because of her gender and making her the target of unwanted sexual innuendoes.

The Court determined that an employee does not need to suffer injury to assert a hostile environment claim under Title VII: "So long as the environment would reasonably be perceived, and is perceived, as hostile or

[31] 499 U.S. at 202.

[32] See *Dothard v. Rawlinson*, 433 U.S. 321 (1977) (Court found sex to be a BFOQ because the employment of a female guard in a maximum-security male penitentiary could create a risk of violence and jeopardize the safety of inmates); *Western Airlines, Inc. v. Criswell*, 472 U.S. 400 (1985) (Court found age to be a BFOQ in an ADEA case because the employment of an older flight engineer could cause a safety emergency and jeopardize the safety of passengers).

[33] 510 U.S. 17 (1993).

abusive...there is no need for it also to be psychologically injurious."[34] While the Court recognized that a standard based on the perceptions of a reasonable person is not "mathematically precise," it emphasized both the need to consider all of the circumstances and the fact that Title VII does not require concrete psychological harm.[35] The Court identified four factors that should be considered to determine whether a hostile environment exists: (1) the frequency of the discriminatory conduct; (2) the severity of such conduct; (3) whether the conduct is physically threatening or humiliating; and (4) whether the conduct interferes unreasonably with an employee's work performance.[36] Although the Court recognized these factors as those to be considered in identifying a hostile environment, it emphasized that no single factor is determinative.

The Court continued its examination of hostile environment sexual harassment in two cases involving vicarious liability. In *Faragher v. City of Boca Raton,* the Court found that an employer is vicariously liable for actionable discrimination caused by a supervisor, subject to an affirmative defense that must consider the reasonableness of the employer's conduct, as well as the conduct of the employee.[37] The petitioner, a former lifeguard for the Marine Safety Section of Boca Raton's Parks and Recreation Department, alleged that she was subject to an environment characterized by lewd remarks, gender-biased speech, and uninvited and offensive touching by her former supervisors.

The petitioner pursued three lines of reasoning drawn from agency law to argue that the City was vicariously liable for the hostile environment created by the supervisors. First, the petitioner contended that the supervisors were acting within the scope of their employment when they engaged in the harassing conduct. Second, the petitioner argued that in creating a hostile environment the supervisors were aided by their supervisor authority. Third, the petitioner claimed that the City was negligent for failing to prevent the harassment by the supervisors.

In addressing the petitioner's first argument, the Court conceded that a supervisor is responsible for maintaining a productive and safe work environment. However, the Court also contended that it was unlikely that

[34] 510 U.S. at 22.

[35] *Id.*

[36] 510 u.S. at 23.

[37] 542 U.S. 775, 118 S. Ct. 2275 (1998).

Congress wished courts to ignore the traditional distinction between acts falling within the scope of employment and those amounting to what "older law" recognized as frolics or detours.[38] The Court concluded that when a supervisor expresses his sexual interests "in ways having no apparent object whatever of serving an interest of the employer," such harassment should be classified as beyond the scope of employment and should not impose liability on the employer.[39] Further, the Court stated that if employers were liable for the hostile environments created by supervisors under a "scope of employment" theory, it would be just as appropriate to find liability when such an environment was created by co-workers. The Court expressed reluctance to recognize such liability.

Although the Court rejected the petitioner's cope of employment argument, it was persuaded that the supervisors were aided in creating a hostile environment by their superior positions. The Court recognized that the authority conferred as a result of a supervisor's relationship with the employer allows the supervisor greater ability to act inappropriately: "When a person with supervisory authority discriminates in the terms and conditions of subordinates' employment, his actions necessarily draw upon his superior position over the people who report to him...whereas an employee generally cannot check a supervisor's abusive conduct the same way that she might deal with abuse from a co-worker."[40]

While the Court recognized that there could be vicarious liability for the misuse of supervisory authority, it established the availability of an affirmative defense for employers. This affirmative defense would consist of the employer's assertion that it exercised reasonable care to prevent and correct any sexually harassing behavior. In addition, the affirmative defense would maintain that the employee unreasonably failed to take advantage of any preventive or corrective opportunities provided by the employer. The Court believed that the employer's ability to assert such an affirmative defense was consistent with Title VII's objective of encouraging employers to prevent sexual harassment from occurring.[41]

After applying its new rule to the case at bar, the Court concluded that the City did not exercise reasonable care to prevent the supervisors' harassing

---

[38] 118 S.Ct. at 2288.
[39] 118 S.Ct. at 2289.
[40] 118 S.Ct. at 2291.
[41] 118 S.Ct. at 2292.

conduct. Although the City maintained a policy against sexual harassment, it failed to disseminate that policy to beach employees. Further, the City made no attempt to monitor the conduct of the supervisors or assure employees that they could bypass harassing supervisors to register complaints.

The Court addressed briefly the petitioner's third argument of the City's negligence by contending that the regulations of the Equal Employment Opportunity Commission (EEOC) require that employers take steps to prevent Title VII violations. The existence of such regulations established that the City had a duty to prevent the harassment. Although the City did adopt an antiharassment policy in 1986, it failed to implement the policy with respect to beach employees.

The Court revisited the issue of vicarious liability for employers in *Burlington Industries v. Ellerth*, a companion case to *Faragher.*[42] In *Burlington Industries,* the Court maintained that an employer may be found vicariously liable for harassment by a supervisor even if the employee suffers no adverse, tangible job consequences.

The petitioner in *Burlington Industries* alleged that she was subjected to repeated offensive remarks and gestures by a mid-level manager who supervised the petitioner's immediate supervisor. On three occasions, the manager made remarks that could be construed as threat to deny the petitioner job benefits. For example, the manager encouraged the petitioner to "loosen up" because he "could make [her] life very hard or very easy at Burlington."[43] Although Burlington maintained a policy against sexual harassment, the petitioner did not inform anyone in authority about the manager's misconduct. Instead, the petitioner resigned from her position, providing reasons unrelated to the harassment. Three weeks after her resignation, the petitioner informed Burlington of her true reasons for leaving.

While the manager's threats suggested that the claim should be analyzed as a quid pro quo claim, the Court categorized it as a hostile environment claim because it involved only unfulfilled threats. After reviewing the petitioner's claim in terms similar to *Faragher,* the Court determined that the manager at Burlington also misused his supervisory authority. The Court concluded that Burlington should be given the opportunity to assert and prove an affirmative defense to liability.

---

[42] 524 U.S. 742, 118 S.Ct. 2257 (1998).

[43] 118 S.Ct. at 2262.

The availability of punitive damages for violations of Title VII was recently addressed by the Court in *Kolstad v. American Dental Association.*[44] In *Kolstad,* the Court continued to build on its holdings in *Faragher* and *Burlington Industries* by concluding that although an employer may be vicariously liable for the misconduct of its supervisory employees, it will not be subject to punitive damages if it has made good faith efforts to comply with Title VII. The Court noted that subjecting employers that adopt antidiscrimination policies to punitive damages would undermine Title VII's objective of encouraging employers to prevent discrimination in the workplace.

SAME-SEX SEXUAL HARASSMENT

In 1998, the Court interpreted Title VII's prohibition against discrimination "because of...sex" to include harassment involving a plaintiff and defendant of the same sex.[45] The petitioner in *Oncale v. Sundowner Offshore Services, Inc.* alleged that he was physically assaulted in a sexual manner and was threatened with rape by three male-co-workers.[46] Two of the co-workers had supervisory authority over the petitioner.

Although the Court acknowledged that Congress was "assuredly" not concerned with make-on-male sexual harassment when it enacted Title VII, it found no justification in the statutory language or the Court's precedents for excluding same-sex harassment claims from the coverage of Title VII.[47] At the same time, the Court stated that inquiries in same-sex harassment cases require careful consideration of the social context in which particular behavior occurs and is experienced by the claimant. For example, the Court distinguished a football player being patted on the butt in a locker room from similar behavior occurring in an office. The Court contended that this kind of consideration would prevent Title VII from becoming a "general civility code" for the American workplace.[48]

---

[44] No. 98-208, 1999 WL 407481 (U.S. June 22, 1999).
[45] 42 U.S.C. § 2000e-2.
[46] 523 U.S. 75, 77 (1998).
[47] 523 U.S. at 79.
[48] 523 U.S. at 80.

TITLE IX OF THE EDUCATION AMENDMENTS OF 1972

Title IX of the Education Amendments of 1972 prohibits discrimination on the basis of sex in educational programs and activities that receive federal funding. Until recently, Title IX claims have been most common among women and girls challenging inequities in sports programs.[49] Title IX is now used as a vehicle for challenging sexual harassment in classrooms and on campuses.

Title IX provides, in relevant part, that "[n]o person in the United States shall, on the basis of sex, be excluded from participation in, be denied the benefits of, or be subjected to discrimination under any education program or activity receiving Federal financial assistance..."[50] The Court's recent decisions involving Title IX address various issues, including the availability of damages and who may be subject to liability.

In *Franklin v. Gwinnett County Public Schools*, a student in the Gwinnett County School District sought monetary damages for violation of Title IX.[51] The petitioner argued that she had been subjected to continual sexual harassment and abuse by a teacher employed by the school district. Although the harassment became known and an investigation was conducted, teachers and administrators did not act and the petitioner was subsequently discouraged from pressing charges. Following *Meritor Sav. Bank, FSB v. Vinson*, the case in which the Court first recognized hostile environment sexual harassment as a cognizable claim under Title VII, the Court in *Franklin* concluded that when a teacher sexually harasses and abuses a student, the teacher discriminates similarly on the basis of sex.[52]

The Court contended that absent clear direction to the contrary, the federal courts could award any appropriate relief in an action brought pursuant to a federal statute. Thus, because Title IX was silent on the issue of monetary damages, the Court found that they were available for the student.

In *Gebser v. Lago Vista Independent School District,* the Court determined that a school district will not be held liable under Title IX for a

[49] See also Kimberly Jones, *Sexual Harassment in Education: Recent Legal Developments Under Title IX of the Education Amendments of 1972*, CRS Report 98-798 A.

[50] 20 U.S.C. § 1681(a).

[51] 503 U.S. 60 (1992).

[52] 503 U.S. at 75.

teacher's sexual harassment of a student if the school district did not have actual notice of the harassment and did not exhibit deliberate indifference to the misconduct.[53] The petitioner, a female high school student, was involved in a sexual relationship with one of her teachers. Unlike the situation in *Franklin*, the school district did not have actual notice of any sexual relationship between the petitioner and the teacher until they were discovered by a police officer. The principal of the petitioner's school did learn of inappropriate comments made by the teacher prior to the discovery, but he cautioned the teacher about such comments. After the sexual relationship became known, the school district quickly terminated the teacher. Despite the school district's actions, the petitioner argued that the school district should be found liable on the basis of vicarious liability or constructive notice.[54]

In requiring the school district to have actual notice of the harassment, the Court discussed the absence of an express course of action under Title IX. Unlike Title VII, Title IX does not address damages or the particular situations in which damages are available.[55] While Title IX does address a denial of funds for noncompliance with its provisions, it does not provide for a private right of action. Instead, a private right of action has been judicially implied.[56]

Because Title IX does not contain any reference to the recovery of damages in private actions, the Court reasoned that its recognition of theories of vicarious liability and constructive notice would allow an unlimited recovery where Congress has not spoken.[57] Stated differently, the Court was reluctant to expand the availability of damages for such theories when Title IX failed to provide initially for a private cause of action. In this way, the Court sought to refine its holding in *Franklin* and limit those situations in which a remedy for damages would lie.

The Court believed that Title IX's remedial scheme would be undermined if it did not require that a school district have actual notice of a teacher's sexual harassment. § 902 of Title IX states that financial assistance will not be denied until the "appropriate person or persons" have been advised of the

---

[53] 524 U.S. 274, 118 S.Ct. 1989 (1998).

[54] Under a theory of constructive notice, liability would be established on the grounds that the school district knew or should have known about the harassment but failed to discover and eliminate it.

[55] 118 S.Ct. at 1996.

[56] See also *Cannon v. University of Chicago,* 441 U.S. 677 (1979).

[57] 118 S.Ct. at 1997.

discrimination and have failed to end the discrimination voluntarily."[58] An "appropriate person" is an official of the entity receiving funds who has the authority to take corrective action.[59] Because the school district in *Gebser* did not have actual notice of the sexual relationship, it could not have taken any steps to end the alleged discrimination.

In addition, the Court stated that damages will not be available unless it is shown that a response exhibits a deliberate indifference to the discrimination; that is, there must be "an official decision by the recipient not to remedy the violation."[60] In *Gebser*, the school district responded to the situation by first cautioning the teacher, and then terminating him once the relationship was discovered. Thus, the Court concluded that the school district did not act with deliberate indifference.

In *National Collegiate Athletic Association v. Smith,* the Court found that a private organization is not subject to Title IX simply because it receives payments from entities that receive federal financial assistance.[61] The respondent, a female graduate student, alleged that the National Collegiate Athletic Association (NCAA) discriminated against her on the basis of sex by denying her permission to play intercollegiate volleyball at two federally assisted institutions. Under NCAA rules, a graduate student is permitted to participate in intercollegiate athletics at only the institution that awarded her undergraduate degree. The respondent graduated from one university, but enrolled at two different universities for her graduate degree. The respondent argued that the NCAA granted more waivers from eligibility restrictions to male graduate students than to female graduate students.

The Court concluded that the NCAA was not a recipient of Title IX funds. The NCAA did not receive federal assistance either directly or through an intermediary. Instead, it received dues payments from member institutions. The Court stated, "[a]t most, the Association's receipt of dues demonstrates that it indirectly benefits from federal assistance afforded its members. This showing, without more, is insufficient to trigger Title IX coverage."[62] Because the Court found that the NCAA was not amenable to suit, it did not address the respondent's substantive allegations of discrimination.

---

[58] See 20 U.S.C. § 1682.

[59] 118 S.Ct. at 1999.

[60] *Id.*

[61] No. 98-84, 1999 WL 83907 (U.S. Feb 23, 1999).

[62] 199 WL 83907 at 5.

Recently, the Court recognized student-student sexual harassment as a cognizable claim under Title IX. In *Davis v. Monroe County Board of Education*, a mother alleged that her daughter suffered discrimination as a result of the Monroe County Board of Education's ("Board") failure to respond to the misconduct of another student.[63] While LaShonda, the petitioner's daughter, was in the fifth grade, a male student allegedly made vulgar remarks to her and touched her in inappropriate manner. Although the petitioner's and LaShonda notified the principal and several teachers, the misconduct continued. The male student was never disciplined for his actions. In addition, no effort was made to separate LaShonda and the male student in classes. The petitioner alleged that LaShonda's grades dropped as a result of the harassment. It appears that LaShonda also contemplated suicide because of the male student's continued misconduct.[64]

The Board maintained that the Court should not find a private damages action under Title IX for student-on-student harassment because the statute proscribes only misconduct by grant recipients. Title IX was enacted pursuant to Congress's pending power. In interpreting such spending legislation, courts have generally insisted that recipients of federal funding have adequate notice of misconduct that could jeopardize their funding.[65] Because Title IX proscribes only misconduct by grant recipients, the Board argued that it did not have notice of a possible claim for misconduct by a third party.

However, the Court maintained that a private damages action could exist, when a funding recipient intentionally violates the clear intent of Title IX. In *Gebser*, for example, the Court determined that a school district could be liable for the misconduct of a teacher if the school district remained deliberately indifferent to the misconduct. Here, LaShonda's school knew about the harassment and did nothing to address it. In addition, the Court contended that the federal regulatory scheme surrounding Title IX and existing tort law provide examples of schools being liable for the misconduct of third parties. Thus, there was adequate notice that such misconduct could result in liability.

The Court concluded that recipients of federal funding may be liable for subjecting their students to discrimination where the recipient is deliberately indifferent to know acts of student-on-student harassment and the harasser is

---

[63] No. 97-843, 1999 WL 320808 (U.S. May 24, 1999)

[64] *Id.* at 4.

[65] 1999 WL 320808 at 7.

under the school's disciplinary authority. In identifying the level of harassment necessary to state an actionable claim, the Court stated that the harassment must be "so severe, pervasive, and objectively offensive that it can be said to deprive the victims of access to the educational opportunities or benefits provided by the school."[66] The Court rejected the possibility of students using Title IX to remedy teasing or name-calling by contending that the misconduct must be serious enough to have a systemic effect of denying the victim equal access to an educational program or activity.

While the development of sex discrimination law under Title IX owes much to Title VII, the *Davis* Court's recognition of student-on-student harassment highlights dramatic differences between the two statutes. As suggested by the dissent in *Davis*, any analogies between student-on-student, harassment cases and Title VII hostile environment cases are inappropriate because "schools are not workplaces and children are not adults."[67] For that reason, any import of Title VII hostile environment analysis should be done with caution.

Further, the dissent recognized that while there is a cap on money damages under Title VII, no such cap exists for private causes of action under Title IX. Thus, a plaintiff could seek damages close to the amount designated originally to a school district. For example, Monroe County received approximately $679,000 in federal aid in 1992-93.[68] Davis sought $500,000 in damages.[69] The dissent maintained that this "limitless liability" under Title IX would put schools in a far worse position than business.[70]

Finally, unlike Title Vii, Title IX has no provision for agency investigation. Thus, Title IX does not contain a mechanism for weeding out frivolous claims and settling meritorious ones at minimal costs. While Congress could consider the creation of an agency like the EEOC to handle

---

[66] 1999 WL 320808 at 14.
[67] 1999 WL 320808 at 27.
[68] 1999 WL 320808 at 32.
[69] *Id.*
[70] 1999 WL 320808 at 32.

initial investigations under Title IX, such action could possible move Title IX closer to Title VII, reducing the distinctions between classroom and workplace.

SEXUAL HARASSMENT AND VIOLENCE AGAINST WOMEN: DEVELOPMENTS IN FEDERAL LAW

Charles V. Dale

INTRODUCTION

Gender-based discrimination, harassment, and violence against women in the home, workplace, and society at large have received increasing legislative and judicial attention in recent years. Legal doctrines condemning the extortion of sexual favors as a condition of employment or job advancement, and other sexually offensive workplace behaviors resulting in a "hostile environment," continue to evolve from judicial decisions under Title VII of the 1964 Civil Right Act and other federal equal employment opportunity laws. In 1994, Congress broke new legal ground by creating a civil rights cause of action for victims of "crimes of violence motivated by gender." The new law also made it a federal offense to travel interstate with the intent to "injure, harass, or intimidate" a spouse, causing bodily harm to the spouse by a crime of violence.[1]

Sexual harassment has also arisen in other legal contexts. The recent military conviction of a drill Sergeant at the Army's Aberdeen training facility for rape and sexual harassment of female recruits, and charges of harassment

---

[1] 18 U.S.C. § 2261(a)(1).

lodged against that branch's highest ranking Sergeant-Major , have focused the public's attention once more upon sexual harassment in the military. Issues surrounding the legal responsibility of school districts or other educational authorities for sexual harassment within the schools are highlighted by judicial decisions and several recently alleged incidents of sexual abuse or unwanted displays of affection involving public school students.

Earlier this term, the U.S. Supreme Court in *Lanier v. United States* reversed a Sixth Circuit decision which had set-aside the conviction of a state judge in Tennessee under 18 U.S.C. § 242 for harassment and sexual assault perpetrated by the judge upon several female court employees and litigants. Section 242, the criminal equivalent of 42 U.S.C. § 1983,penalizes the willful "deprivation of any rights...protected by the Constitution" committed by any person "under color of law." Federal prosecutors claimed that the defendant's acts were committed in his capacity as a judge and that his acts deprived the victims of liberty and bodily integrity protected by the Constitution. The prosecution theory was rejected by the appeals court on the grounds that no right to be free from sexually-motivated physical assault had ever been recognized by a Supreme Court decision involving similar facts. That basis of decision was rejected by a unanimous Supreme Court which remanded the case for additional proceedings. The High Court refrained from deciding the central question, however, of whether it is a federal "constitutional crime" under § 242 for state officials or persons acting under "color of law" to deprive another of "bodily integrity" through acts of forcible sexual assault. Final resolution of that issue must now await further judicial consideration and possible appeals following remand.

FEDERAL EQUAL EMPLOYMENT OPPORTUNITY LAW

Title VII of the 1964 Civil Rights Act does not mention sexual harassment but makes it unlawful for employers with 15 or more employees to discriminate against any applicant or employee "because of...sex."[2] Federal law on the subject is, therefore, largely a judicial cretin, having evolved over nearly a three-decade period from federal court decisions and guidelines of the

[2] 42 U.S.C. § 2000e-2(a)(1).

Equal Employment Opportunity Commission (EEOC) interpreting Title VII's sex discrimination prohibition.[3] Two forms of sexual harassment are forbidden by current Title VII caselaw and EEOC administrative guidelines. The first, or *quid pro quo"* harassment, occurs when submission to "unwelcome" sexual advances, propositions, or other conduct of a sexual nature is made an express or implied condition of employment, or where it is used as the basis of employment decisions affecting job status or tangible employment benefits. As its name suggests, this form of harassment involves actual or potential economic loss—e.g. termination, transfer, or adverse performance ratings, *etc.*—as a consequence of the employee's refusal to exchange sexual favors demanded by a supervisor or employer for employment benefits. The second form of actionable harassment consists of unwelcome sexual conduct which is of such severity as to alter a condition of employment by creating an "intimidating, hostile or offensive working environment." The essence of a "hostile environment" claim is a "pattern or practice" of offensive behavior by the employer, a supervisor, co-workers, or non-employees so "severe or pervasive" as to interfere with the employee's job performance or create an abusive work environment.

In 1980, the federal agency responsible for enforcing Title VII issued interpretative guidelines prohibiting bout *quid pro quo* and hostile environment sexual harassment. The EEOC guidelines focus on sexuality rather than gender—in terms of job detriments resulting from "[u]nwelcome sexual advances, requests for sexual favors, and other verbal or physical behavior of a sexual nature"—and require that a "totality of the circumstances" be considered to determine whether particular conduct constitutes sexual harassment.[4] In addition, judicial developments in hostile environment law were anticipated by elimination of tangible economic loss as a factor and by providing that unwelcome sexual conduct violates Title VII

---

[3] 42 U.S.C. 2000e *et seq*. Sexual harassment in federally assisted education programs is also prohibited by Title IX of the 1972 Education Amendments, 20 U.S.C. §§ 1681 *et seq.* (*Franklin v. Gwinnet County Public Schools,* 503 U.S. 60 (1992). While Title VII and Title IX are the primary sources of federal sexual harassment law, relief from such conduct has also been sought, *albeit* less frequently, pursuant to § 1983 of Title 42, the Federal Employees Liability Act, and the Equal Protection and Due Process Clauses of the U. S. Constitution *E.g. Doe v. Taylor Independent School District,* 975 F. 2d 137 (5th Cir. 1992)(holding that a student has a firmly established equal protection and due process right to be free form sexual molestation by a state-employed school teacher).

[4] 29 C.F.R. § 1604.11(a)(1995).

whenever it "has the purpose of effect of unreasonably interfering with an individual's work performance or creating an intimidating, hostile, or offensive working environment." According to the EEOC guidelines, an employer is liable for both forms of sexual harassment when perpetrated by supervisors.[5] The employer, however, is liable for harassment when perpetrated by coworker or nonemployees only if the employer knew or should have known of the harassment and failed to "take immediate and appropriate corrective action."[6] They also recommend that employers take preventive measures to eliminate sexual harassment[7] and state that employers may be liable to those denied employment opportunities or benefits given to another employee because of submission to sexual advances.[8]

On March 19, 1990, the EEOC issued "Policy Guidance on Sexual Harassment" to elaborate on certain legal principles set forth in its interpretative guidelines from a decade before.[9] First, the later document reasserts the basic distinction between "quid pro quo" and "hostile environment" and states that an employer "will always be held responsible for acts of '*quid pro quo*' harassment" by a supervisor while hostile environment cases require "careful examination" of whether the harassing supervisor was acting in an 'agency capacity'".[10] On the "welcomeness" issue, the policy guide states that "a contemporaneous complaint or protest" by the victim is an "important" but "not a necessary element of the claim." Instead, the Commission will look to all "objective evidence, rather than subjective, uncommunicated feelings" to "determine whether the victim's conduct is consistent, or inconsistent, with her assertion that the sexual conduct is unwelcome."[11] In determining whether a work environment is hostile, several factors are emphasized:

(1) whether the conduct was verbal or physical or both;
(2) how frequently it was repeated;
(3) whether the conduct was hostile and patently offensive;

---

[5] *Id.* at § 1604.11(c).
[6] *Id.* at § 1604.11(d)-(e) (1995).
[7] *Id.* at § 1604.11(f).
[8] *Id.* at § 1604.11(g).
[9] BNA, FEP Manual 405:6681 *et seq.*
[10] *Id.* at 405:6695.
[11] *Id.* at 405:6686.

(4) whether the alleged harasser was a co-worker or a supervisor;
(5) whether others joined in perpetrating the harassment; and
(6) whether the harassment was directed at more than one individual.[12]

However, because the alleged misconduct must "substantially interfere" with the victim's job performance, "sexual flirtation or innuendo, even vulgar language that is trivial or merely annoying, would probably not establish a hostile environment."[13] In addition "the harasser's conduct should be evaluated from the objective standard of a 'reasonable person.'"[14]

QUID PRO QUO HARASSMENT

The earliest judicial challenges involving tangible benefit or *quid pro quo* harassment claims—filed by women who were allegedly fired for resisting sexual advances by their supervisors—were largely unsuccessful. The discriminatory conduct in such cases was deemed to arise from "personal proclivity" of the supervisor rather than "company directed policy which deprived women of employment opportunities." Until the mid-1970's federal district courts were reluctant either to find a Title VII cause of action or to impose liability on employers who were neither in complicity with, nor with actual knowledge of, *quid pro quo* harassment by their supervisory employees. An historic turning point came when the federal district court in *Williams v. Saxbe*[16] held for the first time that sexual harassment was discriminatory treatment within the meaning of Title VII because "it created an artificial barrier to employment which was placed before one gender and not the other, despite the fact that both genders were similarly situated."[16] Echoing earlier opinions that an employer is not liable for "interpersonal disputes between employees," the court nonetheless refused to dismiss the complaint since "if [the alleged harassment] was a policy or practice of

[12] *Id.* at 405:6689.
[13] *Id.*
[14] *Id.*
[16] *Id.* at 657-58.
[16] *Id.* at 657-58.

plaintiff's supervisor, then it was the agency's policy or practice, which is prohibited by Title VII."[17]

Appellate tribunals in several federal circuits soon began to affirm that *quid pro quo* harassment violates Title VII where "gender is a substantial factor in the discrimination." Reversing contrary lower court holdings. For example, Judge Spotswood Robinson, writing for the D.C. Circuit in *Barnes v. Costle*[18] disagreed with "the notion that employment conditions summoning sexual relations are somehow exempted from the coverage of Title VII" as implied by the decision below. Finding that it was "enough that gender is a factor contributing to the discrimination in a substantial way," Judge Robinson ruled that differential treatment based upon an employee's rejection of her supervisor's sexual advances violated the statute. Similarly, in *Tomkins v. Public Service Electric & Gas CO.,* the Third Circuit reversed the trial court's denial of Title VII protection to all "sexual harassment and sexually motivated assault," finding that where an employee's "status as a female was a motivating factor in the supervisor's conditioning her continued employment on compliance with his sexual demands," actionable *quid pro quo* harassment had occurred. "[T]o establish a *prima facie* case of *quid pro quo* harassment, a plaintiff must present evidence that she was subject to unwelcome sexual conduct, and that her reaction to that conduct was then used as the basis for decisions affecting the compensation, terms, conditions, or privileges or her employment."[19] And while the loss of a "tangible employment benefit" has most often mean dismissal or demotion, *quid pro quo* claims may also arise from denial of career advantages—job title, duties or assignments—of less immediate economic impact upon the employee. The Seventh Circuit, for example, ruled recently that a tenured professor who was allegedly stripped of her job title and removed from academic committees because she rebuffed the sexual advances of the university provost may have a claim for *quid pro quo* sexual harassment under Title VII.[20]

---

[17] *Id. at 660-61.*

[18] 561 F.2d 983 (D.C. Cir. 1997)

[19] *Karibian v. Columbia University,* 14 F.3d 773, 777 (2nd Cir.), *cert, denied,* 114 S.Ct. 2693 (1994).

[20] *Bryson v. Chicago Sate University,* 1996 U.S. App. Lexis 24652 (7th Cir. 9-18-96).

HOSTILE ENVIRONMENT HARASSMENT AND THE COURTS

The earlier judicial focus on economic detriment or *quid pro quo* harassment—making submission to sexual demands a condition to job benefits—has largely given way to Title VII claims for harassment that creates an "intimidating, hostile, or offensive environment." The first federal appellate court to jettison the tangible economic loss requirement and recognize a hostile environment claim of sexual harassment was the D.C. Circuit n *Bundy v. Jackson.*[21] The plaintiff there charged that several supervisors made continual sexual advances and propositions, questioned her about her sexual proclivities, ignored her complaints, criticized her work performance, and attempted to block her bid for promotion. The appeals court ruled that actionable sex discrimination is not limited to gender-based conditions resulting in a tangible job consequence, but occurs whenever sex is a motivating factor in treating an employee in an adverse manner. Despite the plaintiff's failure to prove *quid pro quo* harassment—she was not fired, demoted, or denied a promotion—the court was unwilling to adopt a rule that would permit an employer to lawfully harass an employee "by carefully stopping short of firing the employee or taking any other tangible actions against her in response to her resistance."[22] Another decision important to the judicial development of sexually hostile environment law was *Henson v. Dundee* where the Eleventh Circuit rejected a claim of *quid pro quo* harassment but found that the employee had a right to a trial on the merits to determine whether the misconduct alleged made her job environment hostile.[23]

---

[21] 641 F.2d 934 (1981).

[22] *Id.* at 945.

[23] 682 F.2d 897 (11th Cir. 1982). In an oft-quoted passage from its opinion, the court stated:

> Sexual harassment which creates a hostile or offensive environment for members of one sex is every bit the arbitrary barrier to sexual equality at the workplace that racial harassment is to racial equality. Surely, a requirement that a man or woman run a gauntlet of sexual abuse in return for the privilege of being allowed to work and make a living can be as demeaning and disconcerting as the harshest of racial epithets. A pattern of sexual harassment inflicted upon an employee because of her sex is a pattern of behavior that inflicts disparate treatment upon a member of one sex with respect to terms, conditions, or privileges of employment. There is no requirement that an employee subjected to such disparate treatment prove in addition that she suffered tangible job detriment. *Id.* at 902.

Meritor Savings Bank v. Vinson[24] ratified the consensus then emerging among the federal circuits by recognizing a Title VII cause of action for sexual harassment. Writing for the Supreme Court in 1986, then-Justice Rehnquist affirmed that a "hostile environment," predicted on "purely psychological aspects of the workplace environment," could give rise to legal liability and that "tangible loss" of "an economic character' was not an essential element. This holding was qualified by the Court with important reservations drawn from earlier administrative and judicial precedent. First,

> "not all workplace conduct that can be described as 'harassment' affects a term, condition, or privilege of employment within the meaning of Title VII." For example, the "mere utterance" of an "epithet" engendering "offensive feelings in an employee" would not ordinarily be *per se* actionable, the opinion suggests. Rather, the misconduct "must be sufficiently severe or pervasive to alter the conditions of [the victim's] employment and create an abusive working environment."[25]
>
> second, while "voluntariness" in the sense of consent is not a defense to a sexual harassment charge,

[t]he gravamen of any sexual harassment claim is that the alleged sexual advances were 'unwelcome'....The correct inquiry is whether respondent by her conduct indicated that the alleged sexual advances were unwelcome, not whether her actual participation in sexual intercourse was voluntary.[26]

Accordingly, "it does not follow that a complainant's sexually provocative speech or dress is irrelevant as a matter of law in determining whether he or

---

[24] 477 U.S. 57 (1986).

[25] *Id.* at 62 (quoting *Henson v. Dundee), supra* n. 21 at 904. In *Vinson* the complainant alleged that her supervisor demanded sexual relations over a three-year period, fondled her in front of other employees, followed her into the women's restroom and exposed himself to her, and forcibly raped her several times. She claimed she submitted for fear of jeopardizing her employment. During the period she received several promotions which, it was undisputed, were based on merit alone so that no exchange of job advancement for sexual favors (*quid pro quo* harassment) was alleged or found.

[26] *Id.* at 68 (citing 29 C.F.R. § 1604.11(a)(1985).

she found particular sexual advances unwelcome. To the contrary, such evidence is obviously relevant."[27]

Finally, turning to the issue of employer liability, the *Vinson* majority held that the court below had "erred in concluding that employers are always automatically liable for sexual harassment by their supervisors."[28] The usual rule in Title VII cases is strict liability, and four Justices, concurring in the judgment, argued that the same rule should apply in the sexual harassment context as well. The majority disagreed, impliedly suggesting that in hostile environment cases no employer, at least none with a formal policy against harassment, should be made liable in the absence of actual or constructive knowledge.[29]

The Supreme Court's failure to clearly define what constitutes a hostile environment in *Meritory Savings* led to frequent conflict in the lower courts. For example, three federal Circuit Courts of Appeals—the Sixth, the Seventh, and the Eleventh—concluded that in a sexual harassment case, a plaintiff must not only prove that the conduct complained of would have offended a reasonable victim and that he or she was actually offended, but also that the plaintiff suffered serious psychological injury as a result of the conduct.[30] On the other hand, three other Circuits, the Third, the Eighth, and the Ninth, held that the Title VII plaintiff need demonstrate only that he or she was actually offended by conduct that would be deemed offensive by a reasonable victim.[31]

Harris v. Forklift Systems, Inc., [32] revisited and offered some clarification of *Meritor Savings.* The Supreme Court granted certiorari in *Harris* to resolve the conflict among the circuits over whether harassing conduct must produce severe psychological harm to create an actionable hostile environment under

---

[27] *Id.* at 69.

[28] *Id.* at 72.

[29] On the issue of employer liability, *Meritor* states:

[While} declin[ing] the parties' invitation to issue a definitive rule on employer liability...we do agree with the EEOC that Congress wanted courts to look to agency principles for guidance in this area. While such common-law principles may not be transferable in all their particulars to Title VII, Congress' decision to define 'employer' to include any 'agent' of an employer, 42 U.S.C. § 2000e(b), surely evinces an intent to place some limits on the acts of employees for which employers under Title VII are to be held responsible. *Id.* at 72-73.

[30] *Rabidue v. Osceola Refining Co.,* 805 F.2d 611 (6th Cir. 1986); *Scott v. Sears Roebuck,* 789 F.2d 210 (7th Cir. 1986); and *Brooms v. Regal Tube*, 830 F.2d 1554 (11th Cir. 1987).

[31] *Andrews v. City of Philadelphia*, 895 F.2d 1469 (3d Cir 1990); *Burns v. McGregor Electronic Industries, Inc.*, 955 F.2d 559 (8th Cir. 1992); and *Ellison v. Brady,* 924 F.2d 872 (9th Cir. 1991).

[32] 114 S.Ct. 367 (1993).

Title VII. A company president had subjected a female manager to sexual innuendo, unwanted physical touching, and insults because of her gender. After two years, she left the job. Despite its determination that demeaning sexual comments by the employer had "offended the plaintiff, and would offend the reasonable woman," the trial court ruled against the plaintiff since the conduct alleged was not "so severe as to be expected to seriously affect plaintiff's psychological well-being" or create an "intimidating or abusive" environment. The Sixth Circuit upheld the trial court ruling in a three-paragraph unpublished opinion.

The Supreme Court reversed, deciding in 1993 that hostile environment sexual harassment need not "seriously affect psychological well-being" of the victim before Title VII is violated. *Meritor Savings*, wrote Justice O'Connor, had adopted a "middle path" between condemning conduct that was "merely offensive" and requiring proof of "tangible psychological injury." Thus, a hostile environment is not created by the "mere utterance of an...epithet which engenders offensive feelings in an employee.'" On the other hand, a victim of sexual harassment need not experience a "nervous breakdown" for the law to come into play. "So long as the environment would reasonably be perceived and is perceived, as hostile or abusive, there is no need for it also to be psychologically injurious."

Harris also addressed the standards of reasonableness to be applied in judging sexual harassment claims, an issue dividing the lower federal courts then and now. Justice O'Connor opted for a two-part analysis, both components of which must be met for a violation to be found. First, the conduct must create an objectively hostile work environment—"an environment that a reasonable person would find hostile and abusive." Second, the victim must subjectively perceive the environment to be abusive. The "totality of circumstances" surrounding the alleged harassment are to guide judicial inquiry, including "the frequency of the discriminatory conduct; its severity; whether it is physically threatening or humiliating or a mere offensive utterance; and whether it unreasonable interferes with an employee's work performance." Significantly, however, *Harris* did not explicitly resolve a fundamental issue raised by several lower courts regarding the appropriate "gender perspective" to consider in assessing sexual harassment claims.[33]

---

[33] *Compare, e.g. Rabidue v. Osceola Refining Co.,* 805 F.2d 611 622 (6th Cir. 1986)(holding that barrage of "nudie" pictures and litany of degrading comments were "annoying," but would not be sufficiently offensive to a *reasonable person* so as to interfere with the person's work

An increasingly broad range of hostile environment harms—frequently as concerned with lewd comments, inquiries, jokes or displays of pornographic materials in the workplace as with overt sexual aggression—have occupied the federal courts in recent years. *Robinson v. Jackson Shipyards, Inc.*[34] was among the first reported decisions to impose liability for sexual harassment based on the pervasive presence of sexually oriented materials—magazine foldouts or other pictorial depictions—and "sexually demeaning remarks and jokes" by male co-workers without allegations of physical assaults or sexual propositions directed at the plaintiff. Some of the pictures were posted on walls in public view, but included in the category of sexually harassing behavior were incidents where male employees were simply reading the offending magazines in the workplace or carrying them in their back pockets. The district court in *Robinson* rejected the suggestion that sexually oriented pictures or comments standing alone cannot form the basis for Title VII liability, stating that "[e]xcluding some forms of offensive conduct as a matter of law is not consistent with the factually oriented approach" required by Title VII.

Consistent with *Vinson* and *Harris*, however, most courts have limited recovery to cases involving repeated sexual demands or other offensive conduct.[35] Claims involving isolated or intermittent incidents have frequently

---

performance), *cert.denied*, 481 U.S. 1041 (1987) with *Robinson v. Jacksonville Shipyards, Inc.*, 760 F.Supp. 1486, 1524 (M.D. Fla. 1991)(applying *reasonable woman* standard to determine that pervasive pornographic pictures, sexual comments, verbal harassment, abusive graffiti, and unwelcome touching of some of plaintiff's female co-workers created a hostile working environment) and *Spenser v. General Electric Co.,* 697 F. Supp, 204, 218 (E.D. Va. 1988)(finding that sexual comments and suggestive behavior of plaintiff's superior, such as sitting on female workers' laps and talking about private parts, would have seriously affected the psychological well –being of reasonable female employee), *aff'd*, 894 F.2d 651 (4th Cir. 1990). *See also Ellison v,. Brady,* 924 F.2d 872, 879 (9th Cir. 1991)(adopting reasonable woman standard).

34 760 F. Supp. 1486 (M.D. Fla. 1991).

35 E.G. *Highlander v. K.F.C. Nat'l Management Co.*, F. 2d 644 (6th Cir. 1986)(holding that one instance of fondling and one verbal proposition were not sufficient to establish "hostile environment"); *E.g. Waltman v. Int'l Paper Co.*, 875 F.2d 468, 475 (5th Cir. 1989)("focus is whether [plaintiff] was subjected to recurring acts of discrimination, not whether a given individual harassed [plaintiff] recurrently."); *King v. Board of Regents*, 898 F.2d 533, 537 (7th Cir. 1990)("although a single act can be enough ...generally repeated incidents create a stronger claim of hostile environment, with the strength of the claim depending on the number of incidents and the intensity of each incident"). *But of. Vance v. Southern Tel & Tel Co.,* 863 F.2d 1503, 1510 (11th Cir. 1989)("the determination of whether the defendant's conduct is

been dismissed as insufficiently pervasive.[36] For example, the Seventh Circuit recently concluded that while an Illinois state employee "subjectively perceive her work environment to be hostile and abusive" the paucity of sexually oriented comments complained of—three suggestive comments by a co-worker over a three-month period—"were not sufficiently sever that a reasonable person would feel subjected to a hostile working environment."[37] Moreover, except for cases involving touching or extreme verbal behavior, courts are often reluctant to find that sexual derision—or claims against pornography in the workplace—when unaccompanied by sexual demands, is sufficient to create a hostile environment.[38] However, conduct need not be overtly sexual; other hostile conduct directed against the victim because of the victim's sex is also prohibited.[39] Finally, in line with *Vinson,* evidence of a

---

sufficiently 'severe or pervasive' to constitute racial harassment does not turn solely on the number of incidents alleged by plaintiff.").

[36] *Chamberlin v. 101 Realty,* 915 F.2d 777 (1st Cir. 1990)(five mild sexual advances by a supervisor, without more, were insufficient); *Drinkwater v. union Carbide Corp.,* 904 F.2d 853 (3d Cir. 1990)(a claim must demonstrate a "continuous period of harassment and two comments do not create an atmosphere."); *Baskerville v. Culligan Int'l Co.,* 50 F.3d 428, 431 (7th Cir. 1995)(handful of offensive remarks without any physical touching, without any invitations to go out on a date, an without any exposure to pornographic pictures did not constitute sexual harassment); *Ebert v. Lamar Truck Plaza,* 878 F.2d 338 (10th Cir. 1989)(use of foul language and infrequent touching of employee at 24-hour restaurant was not pervasive or severe and management promptly took corrective action whenever complaints were made).

[37] *McKensie v. Illinois Department of Transportation,* 92 F.3d 473 (8th Cir. 1996).

[38] For example, in *Hall v. Gus Construction Co.,* 842 F. 2d 1010, 1017 (8th Cir. 1988), having found that defendants' conduct had gone "far beyond that which even the least sensitive of persons is expected to tolerate," the Eight Circuit nonetheless felt compelled to add that "Title VII does not mandate an employment environment worthy of a Victorian salon. Nor do we expect that our holding today will displace all ribaldry on the roadway." *See also Jones v. Flagship Int'l,* 793 F.2d 714 (5th Cir. 1986)(holding that two requests for sexual contact plus one incident of bare-breasted mermaids as table decorations for a company party were insufficiently pervasive to create hostile environment), *cert, denied,* 479 U.S. 1065 (1987); *Katz v. Dole,* 709 F.2d 251, 256 (4th Cir. 1983)("Title VII is not a clean language act, and does not require employers to extirpate all signs of centuries-old prejudice.").

[39] *See Andrews v. City of Philadelphia,* 898 F.2d 1469, 1485 (3d Cir. 1990)("The Supreme Court [in *Vinson*] in no way limited this concept to intimidation or ridicule of an explicitly sexual nature.");*Bell v. Crackin Good Bakers, Inc.,* 777 F.2d 1497, 1503 (11th Cir. 1985)(holding that valid claim could be based on "threatening, bellicose, demeaning hostile, or offensive conduct by a supervisor in the workplace of the sex of the victim");*McKinney v. Dole,* 765 F.2d 1129, 1140 (D.C. Cir. 1985)(district court erred in assuming that incident of physical force could not constitute sexual harassment unless "explicitly sexual").

sexual harassment claimant's own provocative behavior or prior workplace conduct has generally been deemed relevant to a judicial determination of whether the defendant's conduct was unwelcome.[40]

Of course, a single incident may be actionable if it is linked to a granting or denial of an employment benefit (*quid pro quo* harassment),[41] or if the incident involves physical touching of the employee in an offensive manner under circumstances that preclude her escape.[42] The EEOC policy statement also states that the agency "will presume that the unwelcome, intentional touching of a charging party's intimate body areas is sufficiently offensive to alter the conditions of her working environment and constitute a violation of Title VII."[43]

SAME-SEX HARASSMENT

While the courts and EEOC have interpreted Title VII to protect both men and women against workplace sexual harassment by the opposite sex, it has not been definitely resolved whether the Act's prohibitions apply when the harasser and the victim are of the same sex. The *Meritor* Court found that Congress intended "to strike at the entire spectrum of disparate treatment of men and women" in employment and read Title VII to prohibit discriminatory harassment by a supervisor "because of the subordinate's sex." Although Title VII does not prohibit direct discrimination by an employer based on an employee's sexual orientation[44]—whether homosexual, bisexual, or heterosexual—the EEOC[45] and the District of Columbia,[46] Seventh,[47] Eighth[48]

---

[40] *See e.g., Jones v. Wesco Investments Inc.*, 846 F.2d 1154 n.5 (8th Cir. 1988)("A court must consider any provocative speech or dress of the plaintiff in a sexual harassment case."); *Swentek v. USAIR, Inc.*, 830 F.2d 552, 556 (4th Cir. 1987)(affirming trial judge's determination to permit testimony that the plaintiff was "a foul-mouthed individual who often talked about sex," that the plaintiff had placed a "dildo in her supervisor's mailbox" and once grabbed the genitals of a male co-worker and sexually propositioned him).

[41] *Nelville v. Taft Broadcasting CO.*, 857 F. Supp. 1461 (W.S.N.Y. 1987).

[42] *Barrett v. Omaha National Bank*, 726 F. Supp, 424 (D. Neb. 1983).

[43] BNA, FEP Manual at 405:6681.

[44] *Ulane v. Eastern Airlines, Inc.*, 742 F.2d 1081 (7th Cir. 1984), *cert denied*, 471 U.S. 1017 (1985).

[45] The EEOC Compliance Manual states that the respective sexes of the harasser and the victim are irrelevant in determining whether Title VII has been violated:

and Ninth Circuits[49] have all indicated in dicta that same-sex harassment may be actionable in some circumstances. An apparent majority of federal district courts to consider the issue have also allowed such claims where the alleged harassment is "because of" the victim's sex.[50] The rationale is that Title VII bars disparate treatment based on the sex or gender of the employee, without regard to whether the harasser is male or female.

The Fifth Circuit in *Garcia v. Elf Atochem North America*[51] denied a claim of same-sex harassment under Title VII. *Garcia* held without any analysis that "harassment by a male supervisor against a male subordinate does not state a claim under Title VII even though the harassment has sexual overtones. Title VII addresses gender discrimination."[52] For its conclusion, the Fifth Circuit cited and apparently relied on *Goluszek v. Smith* involving claims by a male that he had been harassed by several male co-workers and that the employer

---

> The victim does not have to be of the opposite sex from the harasser. Since sexual harassment is a form of sex discrimination, the crucial inquiry is whether the harasser treats a member or members of one sex differently from member of the other sex. The victim and the harasser may be of the same sex where, for instance, the sexual harassment is based on the victim's sex (not on the victim's sexual preference) and the harasser does not treat the employees of the opposite sex the same way.

EEOC Compliance Manual, § 615.2(b)(3). While EEOC interpretations of Title VII are not binding on the courts, the are frequently accorded judicial deference. *See Meritor*, 477 U.S. at 65.

46 *Barnes v. Costle,* 561 F.2d 983, 990 n. 55 (D.C. Cir. 1977)(acknowledging the possibility of actionable Title VII claim where "a subordinate of either gender" is harassed "by a homosexual superior of the same gender.").

47 *Baskerville v. Culligan Int's Co.*, 50 F.3d 428, 430 (7th Cir. 1995)(In a heterosexual harassment action, the court noted parenthetically that "sexual harassment of women by men is the most common kind, but we do not mean to excluded the possibility that sexual harassment of men by women, or men by other women would not be actionable in appropriate cases.").

48 *Quick v. Donaldson Co.,* 71 FEP Cases 551 (8th Cir. 1996)(evidence that male employees were the sole targets of other heterosexuals who practice "bagging" co0workers testicles could lead to finding that such treatment was based on sex).

49 *Steiner v. Showboat Operating CO.*, 25 F.3d 1459, 1464 (9th Cir, 1994)(Commenting that "we do not rule out the possibility that both men and women...have viable claims against [a male supervisor] for sexual harassment"), *cert. Denied* 115 S. Ct. 733 (1995).

50 *See Gerd v. United Parcel Service, Inc.,* 1996 U.S. Dist. LEXUS 12180 (D.Colo. 8-19-96) and cases cited therein.

51 28 F.3d 449 (5th Cir. 1994).

52 *Id.* at 451-52 (quoting *Giddens v. Shell Oil Co.,* 12 F.3d 208 (5th Cir. 1993).

failed to remedy the situation after repeated complaints. The *Goluszek v. Smith* involving claims by a male that he had been harassed by several male co-workers and that the employer failed to remedy the situation after repeated complaints. The *Glouszek* court refused "a wooden application of the verbal formulations created by the courts" to salvage same-sex harassment claims, instead focusing on Title VII's concern for "imbalance" and "abuse" of power in the workplace, and the sense of inferiority and "degradation" that results from attacking the sexuality of a "discrete and vulnerable group." Title VII harassment claims are limited, said the court, to the "exploitation of a powerful position to impose sexual demands or pressures on an unwilling but less powerful person." Because the plaintiff was a male in a "male – dominated" work environments, the harassment in question was not "anti-male" or of a kind which treated males as "inferior." *Garcia* and *Goluszek* have been followed by other courts holding that "same-sex harassment is not actionable under Title VII" because the statute "is aimed at a gender-biased atmospheres; an atmosphere of oppression by a 'dominant' gender."[53]

A distinction was drawn by the Fourth Circuit between same-sex harassment predicated on heterosexual and homosexual conduct. In *McWilliams v. Fairfax County Board of Supervisors,*[54] the appeals court refused to recognize same sex harassment under Title VII when neither party was alleged to be homosexual. The opinion focused on Title VII requirement that the discrimination occur "because of the [victim's] sex." This causation requirement could not be met, in the court's view, where the conduct complained of was between heterosexual males because it was not abused on the employee's sex. The denial of relief was limited to heterosexual males in hostile environment cases, however, and "does not purport to reach any form of same-sex discrimination claims where either victim or oppressor, or both, are homosexual or bisexual." To the contrary is the Eighth Circuit's recent decision in *Quick v. Donaldson Co.*[55] which reversed a determination by the district court that the alleged harassment involving heterosexual male employees was not gender-based because the underlying motive was personal enmity or hooliganism.

---

[53] *Vandevanter v. Wabash Nat'l Corp.* 867 F. Supp 790 (N.D. Ind. 1994). See, also *Hopkins v. Baltimore Gas & Electronic Co.,* 871 F. Supp. 882 (D.Md. 1994).

[54] 72 F. 3d 1191 (4th Cir. 1996).

[55] 90 F.3d 1372 (8th Cir. 1996).

On the opening day of its 1996-97 Term, the U.S. Supreme Court left the lower federal courts adrift over the legal status of same-sex harassment when it denied review in *McWillams,*[56] and in another case from the Sixth Circuit involving the dismissal of a male-on-male harassment claim because the facts alleged failed to demonstrate actual or constructive knowledge on the part of the employer.[57] The Court also refused the appeal of a third ruling, *Hopkins v. Baltimore Gas and Electric Co.,*[58] where the Fourth Circuit ruled that the same sex misconduct alleged was not of such severity as to create a hostile work environment under Title VII.

REMEDIES

One major aspect of the 1991 Civil Rights Act[59] of particular importance to sexual harassment claimants was the extension of jury trials and compensatory and punitive damages as remedies for Title VII violations. Previously, Title VII plaintiffs had no right to a jury trial and were entitled only to equitable relief in the form of injunctions against future employer misconduct, reinstatement, and limited back pay for any loss of income resulting from any discharge, denial of promotion, or other adverse employment decision. Consequently, victims of alleged sexual harassment were often compelled to rely on state fair employment practices laws,[60] or traditional common law causes of action for assault, intentional infliction of emotional distress, unlawful interference with contract, invasion of privacy, and the like, to obtain complete monetary relief.[61] Section 102 of the 1991 Act[62] altered the focus of federal EEO enforcement from reliance on judicial injunctions, where voluntary conciliation efforts fail, to jury trials, and

---

[56] *McWIlliams supra n. 55, cert. Denied* No.95-1983, 65 U.S.L.W. 3240 (S.Ct. 10-8-96).

[57] *Fleenor v. Hewitt Soap Co.* 81 F.3d 48 (6th Cir.), *cert denied* No. 96-47, 65 U.S.L.W. 3241 (S.Ct 10-8-96).

[58] 77 F.3d 745 (4th Cir. 1995), *cert denied* No. 95-1961, 65 U.S.L.W. 3239 (S.Ct 10-8-96).

[59] Pub L. 102-166, 105 Stat. 1071.

[60] *E.g., Wiring v. Kinney Shoe Corp.,* 448 N.W. 2d. 526, 51 FEP Cases 885 (Minn. Ct. App. 1989), *aff'd in part and rev'd in part on other grounds,* 461 N.W.2d 374 (Minn. Sup.Ct. 1990).

[61] *See e.g. Rojo v. Kliger*, 52 Cal.3d 65, 901 P.2d 373 (Cal. Sup,Ct. 1990); *Baker v. Weyerhauser Co.,* 903 F.2d 1342 (10th Cir. 1990); *Syndex ocrp. V. Dean,* 820 S.W.2d 869 (Tex. App. 1991).

[62] 105 Stat. 1072, 42 U.S.C. § 1981a.

compensatory and punitive damages, in Title VII actions involving intentional discrimination.

Compensatory damages under the 1991 Act include "future pecuniary losses, emotional pain, suffering, inconvenience, mental anguish, loss of enjoyment of life, and other nonpecuniary losses."[63] The compensatory and punitive damages provided by §102 are "in addition to any relief authorized by Section 706(g)" of the 1964 Civil Rights Act.[64] Therefore, plaintiffs may recover damages in addition to equitable relief, including backpay. Punitive damages may also be recovered against private employers where the plaintiff can demonstrate that the employer acted "malice or reckless indifference" to the individual's federally protected rights. Punitive damages are not recoverable, however, against a governmental entity.[65] In cases where a plaintiff seeks compensatory or punitive damages, any party may demand a jury trial.[66]

The damages newly available under the Act are limited by dollar amount, however, according to the size of the defendant employer during the twenty or more calendar weeks in the current or preceding calendar year. The sum of compensatory and punitive damages awarded may not exceed: $50,000 in the case of an employer with more than 14 and fewer than 101 employees; $100,000 in the case of an employer with more than 100 and fewer than 201 employees; $200,000 in the case of an employer with more than 200 and fewer than 501 employees; and $300,000 in the case of an employer with more than 500 employees.[67] In the jury trial cases, the court may not inform the jury of the damage caps set forth in the statute.

This expansion of Title VII remedies may dramatically affect the level of relief available in cases of intentional sex discrimination, where plaintiffs for the first time have the prospect of federal compensatory and punitive damage recoveries and the right to a jury trial. In particular, the Act now provides a monetary remedy for victims of sexual harassment in employment not tied to lost wages.[68] Since harassment of the hostile environment type often occurs

---

[63] 42 U.S.C. § 1981a(b)(3).

[64] *Id.* at § 1981a(a)(1).

[65] *Id.* at § 1981a(b)(1).

[66] *Id.* at § 1981a(c).

[67] *Id.* at § 1981a(b)(3).

[68] Substantial damage awards in sexual harassment cases brought under state law have recently been reported. For example, in *Stockett v. Tolin,* 791 F. Supp. 1526 (S.D. Fla, 1992), a sexually

without economic loss to the employee, in terms of pay or otherwise, critics of the prior law charged that the sexual harassment victim was frequently without any effective federal relief. Title VII plaintiffs may now seek monetary compensation for emotional pain and suffering, and other pecuniary and nonpecuniary losses, caused by sexual harassment. Moreover, federal claims may be joined with pendent state-law claims for damages unlimited by the caps in the federal law or an election made between pursuing state and federal remedies.

Legislation was introduced during the 104th Congress in both the House and Senate to remove the damage caps under the 1991 Act.[69] The Equal Remedies Act of 1995, identical to bills first proposed two years earlier, calls for elimination of the compensatory and punitive damage ceiling for plaintiffs charging intentional discrimination under TitleVII and the Americans with Disabilities Act, thereby affording the same remedies to those claiming sex, religious, and disability discrimination as race discrimination claimants under the Civil Rights Act of 1866.[70] The legislation had earlier been approved by the Senate Labor and Human Resources Committee, but failed to reach the Senate floor. No House action occurred on the measure in either the 103d or 104th Congress.

LIABILITY OF EMPLOYERS AND SUPERVISORS FOR MONETARY DAMAGES

The addition of monetary damages to the arsenal of Title VII remedies has rekindled into an employer's liability for harassment perpetrated by its supervisors and nonsupervisory employees, and of the personal liability of individual harassers. The lower courts have uniformly declared employers

harassed film-studio employee was held entitled not only to front pay and back pay but also to $250,000 in damages for a variety of torts and a $1 million punitive damages award against the dominant owner of the studio. A jury award of $315,000 in damages and attorneys fees was obtained by a sexual harassment plaintiff asserting a claim of assault and intentional infliction of emotional distress in *Syndex Corp. v. Dean,* 820 S.W. 2d 869 Tex.App. 1991). Of course, the amount of such awards under federal law would be subject to the caps currently imposed by the 1991 Act.

[69] H.R. 96, 104th Cong., 1st Sess. (1995); S. 296, 104th Cong., 1st Sess. (1995).

[70] 42 U.S.C. § 1981.

vicariously liable for *quid pro quo* sexual harassment committed by supervisors.[71] By definition, only those with actual authority to hire, promote, discharge or affect the terms and conditions of employment can engage in *quid pro quo* harassment and are held to acts as agents of the employer, regardless of their motivations. *Quid pro quo* harassment is viewed no differently than other forms of discrimination prohibited by Title VII, for which employers have routinely been held vicariously liable. Because Title VII defines employer to include "any agent" of the employer, the statute is understood to have incorporated the principle of *respondeat superior*, in effect holding "employers liable for the discriminatory [acts of]...supervisory employees whether or not the employer knew, should have known, or approved of the supervisor's actions."[72] However, the suggestion in *Meritor Savings Bank* that courts look to agency law in developing liability rules for hostile work environment cases has resulted in a rejection of vicarious liability by most circuit courts confronting hostile work environment claims.

Most courts before and after *Meritor* have made an employer liable for a hostile environment only if it knew or should have known about the harassment and failed to take prompt remedial action to end it. They reason that, unlike *quid pro quo* cases, in which a supervisor exerts actual authority to affect the terms, conditions, or privileges of a subordinate's employment, the supervisor is cloaked with no actual or apparent authority to create a hostile environment. In other words, the employer is directly liable for its own wrongdoing in not stopping harassment of which it was or should have been aware but is not automatically or "strictly" liable for supervisory misconduct.[73] A minority view however, recognizes vicarious liability when the harasser is a supervisor[74] and creates a hostile environment through threats and intimidation.[75] Similarly, an employer without actual or constructive

[71] *See Horn v. Duke Homes*, 755 F.2d 599, 604 (7th Cir. 1985)(noting that all circuits reaching the issue have held employees strictly liable for *quid pro quo* harassment).

[72] *Meritor Savings*, 477 U.S. at 70-71.

[73] *Lipsett v. University of Puerto Rico*, 864 F.3d 103 (3d Ir. 1994); *Waltman v. International Paper Co.*, 875 F.2d 468 (5th Cir. 1989); *Juarez v. Ameritech Mobile Communications, Inc.*, 957 F.2d 317 (7th Cir. 1992); (*Burns v. McGregor Elec. Indus.*, 995 F.2d 559 (8th Cir. 1992); *Ellison v. Brady*, 824 F.2d 872 (9th Cir. 1991).

[74] *Kaufman v. Allied Signal, Ind.*, 970 F.2d 178 (6th Cir.), *cert.denied*, 113 S.Ct. 831 (1992).

[75] *E.g.Karibian v. Columbia University*, 14 F.3d 773, 780 (2d Cir. 1994)(actions of a "supervisor at a sufficiently high level in the hierarchy would necessary be imputed to the company").

knowledge is generally not liable for co-worker harassment since the discriminatory conduct is not within the scope of employment and the employer usually has conferred no authority, real or apparent, to facilitate the harassment.[76]

Similar divisions exist, again because "agents[s]" are included within the Title VII definition of "employer," as to the personal liability of individual supervisors and co-workers for hostile environment harassment or other discriminatory conduct. A majority of federal circuit courts to address the question—the Second,[77] Fifth,[78] Seventh,[79] Ninth,[80] Tenth[81] and Eleventh[82] and District of Columbia[83]—have interpreted agents in the statutory definition as merely incorporating *respondeat superior* and refused to impose personal liability on agents. These courts also note the incongruity of imposing personal liability on individuals while capping compensatory and punitive damages based on employer size, as the statute does, and exempting small businesses that employ less than 15 persons from Title VII altogether. Of the Courts of Appeals, only the Fourth Circuit[84] has extended Title VII liability to supervisors in both their personal capacity where the supervisor exercised significant control over the plaintiff's hiring, firing, or conditions of employment, The First Circuit, the Third Circuit, the Sixth Circuit, and the Eight Circuit have yet to decide the issue, leading to contradictory results among the district courts in those jurisdiction.[85]

Several recent federal circuit court rulings strongly suggest that the most effective defensive strategy for employers to avoid liability for a hostile work environment may be a proactive approach. As noted, even where the conduct

---

[76] *See e.g. Baker v. Weyerhauser Co.*, 903 F.2d 1342 (10th Cir. 1990); *Steele v. Offshore Shipbuilding, Inc.*, 867 F.2d 1311 (11th Cir. 1989); *Swentek v. USAir, Inc.*, 830 F.2d 552 (4th Cir. 1987).

[77] *Tomka v. Seiler Corp., 66 F.3d 1295 (2nd Cir. 1995).*

[78] *Grant v. Loan Star Co.*, 21 F.3d 649 (5th Cir.), *cert.denied*, 115 S.Ct. 574 (1994).

[79] *EEOC v, AIC Sec. Investigations, Ltd.*, 55 F.3d 1276 (7th Cir. 1995).

[80] *Miller v. Maxwell's Int'l Inc.*, 991 F.2d 583 (9th Cir. 1993), *cert. Denied* 114 S. Ct. 1049 (1994).

[81] *Haynes v. Williams,* 88 F.3d 989 (10th Cir. 1991).

[82] *Busby v. City of Orlando,* 931 F.2d 764 (1th Cir. 1991).

[83] *Gary v. Long,* 59 F.3d 1391 (D.C. Cir. 1995), *cert.denied,* 116 S.Ct. 569 (1995).

[84] *See Paroline v. Unisys Corp.*, 879 F.2d 100 (4th Cir. 1989) *rev'd in part, aff'd in relevant part,* 900 F.2d 27 (4th Cir. 1990) *(en banc).*

[85] *See Hernandez v. Wangen*, 1996 U.S. Dist. LEXIS 11533 (D.P.R. 8-1-96) and cases listed therein.

of a supervisor or co-workers creates a hostile environment, the courts will generally not hold the employer responsible unless he or she knew or should have known of the situation and failed to take prompt corrective action and disciple the alleged harasser. Thus, in *MckEnzie v. Illinois Department of Transportation,*[86] the "prompt" and remedial action" taken by the state employer in barring further workplace contacts between the allegedly harassing co-worker and the complainant was held to prevent recovery on a hostile environment claim. Conversely, a federal jury recently awarded $2 million to a former Wal-Mart clerk who claimed that the retailer fostered a hostile work environment by ignoring her reports of sexual harassment by a fellow employee who attacked and threatened her. The compensatory damages, which included recovery for extensive treatment for post-traumatic stress suffered by the employee after the attack, will be reduced to $300,000 in conformity with the "cap" imposed by the 1991 Civil Rights Act.[87]

In addition, the courts are generally reluctant to impose Title VII liability on employers who act "prophylactically" to stem harassing conditions before they begin. This is illustrated by *Gary v. Long*[88] where the D.C. Circuit dismissed a hostile environment lawsuit against the Washington Metropolitan Area Transit Authority (WMATA) as the result of repeated verbal and physical harassment, and eventual rape, of a female employee by a supervisor. Claims of *quid pro quo* harassment were rejected due to lack of economic detriment. Moreover, WMTA escaped liability on the hostile environment claim because it had an "active and firm" policy against the sexual harassment which it publicized through staff notices, seminars, and EEO counselors, and because it maintained detailed grievance procedures for reporting acts of discrimination. Perhaps the most practical lesson for employers is to formulate and communicate to employees a specific policy forbidding workplace harassment; to establish procedures for reporting incidents of harassment that bypass the immediate supervisor of the victim if he or she is the alleged harasser; to immediately investigate all alleged incidents and order prompt

---

[86] 92 F.3d 463 (7th Cir. 1996).

[87] *Holmes v. Wal-Mart Stores Inc.,* F. Supp. (M.D.Fla 1996). *See also Varner v. National Supermarkets Inc.,* F.3d (8th Cir. 1996)(Supermarket chain liable for compensatory damages of $30,000 to female employee harassed by co-worker because supervisor took no corrective action and company policy dictated referral of complaints to human resources department, "in effect require[ing]...supervisor to remain silent notwithstanding his knowledge of the incidents.").

corrective action (including make-whole relief for the victim) when warranted; and to appropriately discipline the harasser.

SEXUAL HARASSEMENT IN THE SCHOOLS

Issues surrounding the legal responsibility of school districts or other educational authorities for sexual harassment within the schools are highlighted by recent media reports of disciplinary proceedings against students for alleged sexual abuse or unwanted displays of affection directed at their peers. On October 7, 1996, the U.S. Supreme Court denied review of an appeal form *Rowinsky v. Bryan Independent School District*[89] where the Fifth Circuit refuse to award damages or injunctive relief against a local school district under Title IX of the 1972 Education Act Amendment for an alleged hostile environment resulting from the misconduct of students. In *Rowinsky*, male students "physically and verbally abused" two eighth grade daughters of the petitioner by "swatting" and "grabbing" them by various private body parts. Despite repeated complaints by the girls to their bus driver, and by the parents to numerous school and district officials, no investigation or corrective action was taken. In denying relief, the Fifth Circuit disapproved of incorporating the hostile environment concept from Title VII into a peer harassment Title IX case. It pointed to the lack of an agency relationship between the school and the harasser and to its view that there is no "power relationship" between the harasser and the victim, so that "[u]nwanted sexual advances of fellow students do not carry the same corrective effect or abuse of power as those made by a teacher, employer, or co-worker."[90] The Court's refusal to hear the *Rowinsky* case may exacerbate differences of opinion that have emerged to date from lower federal court rulings on the issue of school district liability for student-to-student or so-called "peer" sexual harassment.

Title IX provides that "[no] person in the United States shall, on the basis of sex, be excluded from participation in, be denied the benefits or, or be subjected to discrimination under any education program or activity receiving

[88] 59 F. 3d 1391 (D.C. Cir 1995).

[89] 80 F.3d 1006 (5th Cir. 1996), *cert.denied* No. 96-4, (10-9-96).

[90] 80 F.3d at 1015 n.11.

Federal financial assistance."[91] Under the statute, student victims of any form of sex discrimination, including sexual harassment, may file a written complaint with the Office of Civil Rights (OCR)[92] for administrative determination and possible imposition of sanctions—including termination of federal funding—upon the offending educational institution. OCR interprets Title IX as imposing liability on a recipient educational institution if the institution knew, or should have known, that a student was being subjected to hostile environment sexual harassment by other students and fails to take appropriate corrective action. OCR had applied this interpretation in the course of its enforcement activities on numerous occasions since at least 1989,as confirmed on August 14, 1996 when it issued a Title IX policy guidance regarding peer sexual harassment.

Title IX also provides student victims with an avenue of judicial relief. In *Cannon v. University of Chicago,*[93] the Supreme Court ruled that an implied right of action exists under Title IX for student victims of sex discrimination who need not exhaust their administrative remedies before filing suit. However, the availability of monetary damages under Title IX remained uncertain until *Franklin v. Gwinnett County Public Schools.*[94] In *Franklin*, a female high school student brought an action for damages under title IX against her school district alleging that she had been subjected to sexual harassment and abuse by a teacher. The Supreme Court held that damages were available to the sexual harassment victim if she could prove that the school district had intentionally violated Title IX. Since *Franklin*, there has been general agreement among the courts that Title IX prohibits both *quid pro quo* and hostile environment teacher-student harassment and that schools may be held liable on the basis of agency principles applied in the Title VII context, discussed above. There is less judicial consensus, however, regarding legal standards for holding an educational institution liable for a sexually hostile educational environment created by student misconduct of which the institution was or should have been aware.

First, the federal circuit courts disagree as to the obligation on school officials to take prompt and appropriate corrective action to halt student-to-student or "peer" hostile environment harassment. In the first appellate ruling

---

[91] 20 U.S.C. § 1681 (a).
[92] 34 C.F.R. § 100.7(d)(1)(1995).
[93] 441 U.S. 677 (1979).
[94] 112 S.Ct. 1028 (1992).

on point, *Davis v. Monroe County Board of Education,*[95] the Eleventh Circuit concluded that peer harassment in an educational setting may be compared to co-worker harassment and applied Title VII principles to hold a school district potentially liable for its failure to respond adequately to a student-created hostile environment of which it knew or should have known. Several other courts of appeals appear to have aligned themselves with the Eleventh Circuit by assuming, without directly deciding, that Title IX, like Title VII, requires schools to take prompt corrective action in response to known hostile environment harassment by students or other third parties.[96] In apparent conflict with these courts is *Rowinsky* decision which the Supreme Court refused to hear this Term. The Fifth Circuit there held that a school is not liable for mere inattention to peer sexual harassment claims unless it treated male and female harassment victims differently. Rejecting the Title VII standard based on actual or constructive knowledge, the *Rowinsky* court concluded that there must be an act of discrimination by the school itself—beyond condoning the sexual harassment by students—in order to sustain a school's liability for peer sexual harassment. Thus, the court dismissed the eighth grade students' claims that their school's persistent failure to curtail other students repeated sexual assaults, touching and harassment violated Title IX.

Another judicial fault line divides the circuits as regards the nature of proof required to show "intentional discrimination," justifying Title IX monetary damage awards under *Franklin.* One approach is that taken by the Eleventh Circuit in *Davis*[97] which appears to infer motive or intent sufficient to establish damages liability from a school's failure to respond to student complaints of hostile environment harassment. A stricter intent standard was imposed by *Rowinsky,* however, in effect requiring a plaintiff to prove subjective discriminatory motive on the part of educational officials in order

---

[95] 74 F.3d 1186 (11th Cir. 1996).

[96] *Murray v. New York Univ. College of Dentistry*, 57 F.3d 243, 248-50 (2d Cir. 1995)(discussing Title VII standards in analyzing Title IX sexual harassment claim); *Brown v. Hot, Sexy and Safer Products, Inc.*, 68 F.3d 525, 540 (1st Cir. 1995)(applying Title VII principles to Title IX hostile environment sexual harassment claim), *cert.denied* 116 S.Ct. 1044 (1996); and *Clyde K. v. Puyallup School Dist.*, 35 F.3d 1396, 1402 (9th Cir. 1994)("School officials might reasonably be concerned about liability for failing to remedy peer sexual harassment that exposes female students to a hostile educational environment).

[97] 74 F.3d at 793. *See also Murray supra* n. 94, 57 F.3d at 248-49.

to obtain damages for a failed institutional response to charges of peer sexual harassment.[98]

VIOLENCE AGAINST WOMAN ACT

The Violence Against Women Act (VAWA) was enacted by Congress in1994 "to protect the civil rights of gender-motivated violence." It creates a private cause of action under federal law against persons who perpetrate "crime[s] of violence motivated by gender."[99] Specific "crimes of violence" triggering statutory coverage include "State or Federal offenses" that would constitute "a felony against the person…or a felony against the property," as recognized by federal law,[100] and which pose "a serious risk of physical injury to another," whether or not the misconduct alleged ever resulted in actual charges or a prior criminal action. To be actionable under VAWA, however, the complainant has to show that the offense was "motivated by gender," i.e., that the predicate crime was committed "because of gender or on the basis of gender,"[101] and was at lest partially due to "an animus based on the victim's gender." In other words, no cause of action will lie for injury resulting from mere "random" acts of violence, regardless of the gender of the victim, where it is not proven that the perpetrator was gender-motivated.[102]

The enforcement mechanism provided for this new right to be free of gender-related violent crime is a private civil action in federal (or state) court. The prevailing plaintiff in a judicial action may obtain compensatory and punitive damages, injunctive relief, and "such other relief as the court deems appropriate." While predicated upon conduct that is made criminal by other federal and state law provisions, the statute does not require a prior criminal complaint, prosecution, or conviction to establish the elements of a cause of action. No federal administrative scheme is authorized for VAWA

---

[98] 80 F.3d at 1016.

[99] 42 U.S.C. § 13981.

[100] 18 U.S.C. § 16. In effect, the bill incorporates the existing federal criminal code definition of "crime of violence" as predicate for a civil rights violation under VAWA.

[101] *Id.* at § 13981(e)(1).

[102] Under evidentiary standards prescribed by § 13981(e)(1), the complainant must prove gender motivation "by a preponderance of the evidence."

enforcement,[103] nor are additional criminal penalties provided, but parallel civil and criminal proceedings for conduct which constitutes a VAWA offense are not precluded.

VAWA may to some extent overlap and provide supplemental protection to Title VII for women victimized by gender-motivated violence and harassment in the workplace. Title VII applies only to employment but even there excludes the large segment of the national workforce employed by companies and firms with fewer than 15 employees. A condition precedent to a Title VII judicial action is that the complaining employee or applicant first resort to the EEOC administrative process for voluntary negotiation and conciliation of the matter between the parties. Moreover, while the 1991 amendments added provisions for jury trials and compensatory and punitive damage awards in Title VII actions, such relief is limited by monetary "caps" that find no parallel in later law. The element of "violence," however, is not a requisite of the offense under either the Title VII or Title IX.

The new law's statement of purpose anchors the civil rights remedy for gender-motivated violent crime to the "affirmative" power of Congress under the Commerce Clause of the U.S. Constitution and § 5 of the Fourteenth Amendment. Congressional power to prohibit or remedy equal protection or due process violations has historically been limited by judicial construction of the Fourteenth Amendment to "State action" or private conduct actively supported by the state or its agents. The scope of Congress' authority to regulate purely private conduct pursuant to its §5 enforcement powers is constitutionally unsettled, as is the corollary question of the status of purely private action for purposes of application of equal protection and due to process safeguards.[104] Consequently, the Commerce Clause is frequently invoked to support civil rights law like VAWA that protect persons against discriminatory conduct by private persons unaided by the state. However, judicial developments following from the Supreme Court' 1995 decision in *United States v. Lopez*[105] have raised new questions concerning the scope of

[103] This is in contrast to the voluntary negotiation and conciliation procedures of the Equal Employment Opportunity Commission which must be pursued before filing a federal lawsuit seeking relief from sexual harassment in the workplace under Title VII of the 1964 Civil Rights Act. 42 U.S.C. §§ 2000e *et seq.*

[104] *See e.g. U.S. v. Guest*, 338 U.S. 745 (1966); *U.S. v. Price,* 338 U.S. 787 (1966).

[105] 115 S.Ct. 1624 (1995).

Congress' authority to regulate non-economic activities "affecting commerce" by imposition of federal criminal penalties.

In the *Lopez* case, the Supreme Court invalidated, as exceeding Congress' commerce powers, the Gun-Free School Zones Act of 1990[106], which made a federal offense of possessing a firearm within 1,000 feet of a school. As traditionally applied, the Commerce Clause permits Congress to regulate "use of the channels" and "Instrumentalities" of interstate commerce, as well as activities that "substantially affect" its flow. Despite the absence of congressional findings, the Government in *Lopez* claimed that the statute regulated an activity which substantially impacted interstate commerce because possession of firearms in a school zone may result in an increase in violent crimes. Criminal violence, in turn, affects the national economy by increasing insurance costs, reducing the willingness of persons to travel to areas of the country perceived as unsafe, and by diminishing productivity due to impaired student learning environments. The Supreme Court concluded, however, that Congress' constitutional reach since it had "nothing to do with 'commerce' or any sort of economic enterprise, however broadly one might define those terms." [107] The Court rejected the Government's "cost of crime" argument as an overexpansive theory which would permit Congress to "regulate not only all violent crime, but all activities that might lead to violent crime, regard less of how tenuously they relate to interstate commerce.[108] Were this argument successful, the Court reasoned, "it is difficult to perceive any limitation on federal power, even in areas such as criminal law enforcement or education where States historically have been sovereign."[109]

Two federal district courts have reached opposite conclusions regarding the constitutionality of VAWA's civil rights provision based on *Lopez*. In *Doe v. Doe,*[110] the plaintiff alleged a pattern of "systematic and continuous" physical and emotional abuse at the hands of her spouse over a seventeen year period resulting in severe emotional distress, trauma, and depression. The defendant spouse moved to dismiss, claiming that Congress lacked authority under either the Commerce Clause of the Fourteenth Amendment to enact the WAVA remedy for gender-based violence. The federal district court rejected

---

[106] 18 U.S.C. § 922(a)(1)(A).
[107] *Id.* at 1631.
[108] *Id.* at 1632.
[109] *Id.* at 1632.
[110] 929 F. Supp. 608 (D.Conn. 1996).

the motion, however, finding support for Congress' judgment that violence against women was a "rational basis" for the legislation was found in "statistical, medical, and economic data before the Congress" that was lacking in *Lopez.* The Senate Report, for example, indicated that 50% of rape victims leave the work force involuntarily and that "fear of gender-based crimes restricts movement, reduces employment opportunities, increases health expenditures, and reduces consumer spending all of which affect interstate commerce and the national economy.[111] Moreover, VAWA was found to "complement" rather than encroach upon state procedures because it remedied "deficiencies" in existing state and federal legal protections against gender-based violence while preserving traditional state tort remedies. The federal safeguards were further justified, said the *Doe* Court, given the special harm, community unrest, and likelihood of retaliation, provoked by bias-inspired crime.

Conversely, the VAWA claim of a female student at a state university who had allegedly been raped by two male students was rejected in *Brzonkala v. Virginia Polytechnic and State Unviersity.*[112] The district judge there ruled that the "totality of circumstances"—including vulgar statements made by the defendants concerning the assaults and the "gang Rape" aspect of the case—was sufficient to establish the required "gender animus." Since the law was concerned with neither the channels of interstate commerce, nor commodities moving therein, however, the court applied *Lopez* to analyze the conduct prohibited by the statute in terms of its "substantial effect" on commerce. Such effects were found lacking by *Brzonkala.* First, like the *Lopez* statute, VAWA regulated "non-economic" interstate activity" and there was no requirement that an interstate connection be shown in each individual case. The congressional findings and legislative history relied upon by the *Doe* court were insufficient to supply the missing nexus since "[s]howing that something affects the national economy does not suffice to show that it has a substantial effect on interstate commerce." The court noted that family law issues and most criminal issues "affect the national economy substantially" and have "some effect" on interstate commerce, but to equate the two and "extend Congress' power to these issues would unreasonably tip the balance away from the states,'"

---

[111] S.Rep. 138, 103d Cong., 1st Sess. 54 (1993).
[112] 1996 U.S. Lexis 10766 (W.D. Va. 7-26-96).

As noted, Congress is also granted specific power to enforce civil rights remedies pursuant to § 5 Congress has power independent of the courts to identify equal protection and due process violations and to prescribe remedies for constitutional wrongs. The scope of this legislative authority remains undetermined, however, insofar as congressional regulation of private conduct that is unsupported by state action is concerned. The district court in *Brzonkala* read the Supreme Court rulings in *Morgan* and *Guest supra* to preclude extension of Congress' § 5 power to gender-based violent crime not attributable to the state or its agents. Since the remedy prescribed by VAWA runs against the private individual who commits a criminal act, rather than the state criminal justice system, it could not be justified as a remedy for state inaction or inadequate action in prosecuting gender-based violent crime.

> While remedying the state criminal system's deficiencies is a legitimate Fourteenth Amendment concern, VAWA does not address this concern, because VAWA provides no remedy for the deficiencies, It does not provide a remedy to the victim for the denial of the victim's equal protection rights by either undoing or stopping the specific equal protection violation or by compensating the victim for the violation, nor does it provide a remedy against the equal protection violator.

In short, because VAWA provides a remedy against private persons who commit gender-based violence, but does nothing to address deficiencies in state criminal processes regarding prosecution for rape or other violent crimes against women, it was not a proper exercise of Congress' § 5 authority, according to the *Brzonkala* court.

To date, no federal, appellate tribunal has addressed the legal and constitutional issues raised by the VAWA civil action provisions. Such appeals may be anticipated, however, and a ruling by the Supreme Court this term in the *Lanier* case may provide additional guidance.

UNTIED STATES V. LANIER

On March 31, 1997, the U.S. Supreme Court vacated a ruling by the Sixth Circuit U.S. Court of Appeals which had reversed the conviction of David

Lanier, a Tennessee Chancery Court judge, for willful deprivation of federal constitutional "rights, privileges, or immunities" under color of law in violation of 18 U.S.C. § 242. The charges against Lanier stem from allegations that he raped, assaulted, or harassed eight women in his chambers who either worked for the judge, worked with him, or had cases pending before his court. The "right, privilege or immunity" allegedly violated was identified as a Fourteenth Amendment due process guarantee of "bodily integrity"—specifically, the right to be free of sexual assault by a state official. After a trial, Lanier was convicted on two felony and five misdemeanor counts of violating § 242 and was sentenced to a total of 25 years in prison. A panel of the Court of Appeals for the Sixth Circuit affirmed the conviction and sentence, but the full court overturned the decision and granted rehearing *en banc.*[113]

Invoking established rules of construction for criminal statutes, and the Supreme Court ruling in *Screws v. United States,*[114] then *en banc* majority set aside the conviction on the grounds that exiting § 242 precedents failed to adequately notify the public that simple or sexual assault crimes invaded a constitutional right or liberty protected by the statute. To avoid unconstitutional vagueness, a plurality of the *Screws* Court had construed the statute to require proof of "specific intent" to deprive the victim of a right "made specific either by the express terms of the Constitution ...or by decisions interpreting them." The federal government had argued that a due process right to be free of unwarranted assault recognized by lower court decisions in other contexts provided adequate notice of criminal conduct to be punished. But due to the statute's "abstract" nature, and discrepancies among the circuits and federal district courts in their recognition of "new" constitutional rights, Chief Judge Merritt felt that "[o]nly a Supreme Court decision with nationwide application can make specific a right that can result in § 242 liability" and only when the right had been made to apply in "a factual situation fundamentally similar to the one at bar." The *en banc* court conceded the "outrageous" nature of Judge Lanier's conduct, but found that since the Supreme Court had not so ruled in a "fundamentally similar" situation, the supported right to be free of sexual assault could not form the basis for a federal prosecution.

---

[113] 43 F.3d 1033 (6th Cir. 1995).

[114] 325 U.S. 91 (1945).

Writing for a unanimous Supreme Court, Justice Souter faulted the Sixth Circuit for applying too restrictive a standard and for concluding that § 242 could never incorporate "newly-created constitutional rights." The "fair warning" requirement in *Screws* was not "a categorical rule" excluding from the universe of § 242 safeguards any right not specifically identified by prior Supreme Court decisional law. To interpret the statute so restrictively, said the Court, was "unsound," contradicting both the legislative and judicial history of the criminal civil rights provisions and decisional law governing the corollary "clearly established" qualified immunity standard applied b the courts to determine civil liability of state officials under 42 U.S.C. 1983. The "touchstone" for imposing § 242 criminal liability is whether the statute, either standing alone or as construed by the courts at all levels, "made it reasonably clear at the relevant time that the defendant's conduct was criminal." According to Justice Souter, "general statements of the law" could provide "fair and clear warning" and may apply "with obvious clarity," in at least some situations, even though the particular conduct in question had not previously been held unlawful in precisely the same circumstances.

The Supreme Court's disposition of *Lanier* avoided decision of the main substantive issue in the case-that is, the constitutional status of the right to be free from sexual harassment and abuse at the hands of state officials. Other aspects of ruling, however, and its contemporary legal background may suggest the probable legal outcome of the case on remand. First, in a concluding footnote, the Court rejected "as plainly without merit" several arguments—including the unavailability of § 242 to enforce due process rights—made by Judge Lanier and relied upon by the Sixth Circuit to reach its earlier decision. This will presumably complicate the task of defending Judge Lanier's position on remand. In his background discussion of the case, Justice Souter also quotes with seeming approval from the trial judge's instruction to the jury that the Fourteenth Amendment protection of bodily integrity includes "the right to be free from certain sexually motivated physical assaults and coerced sexual battery. This instruction appears to conform to the weight of existing lower federal court precedent, including a Sixth Circuit decision since *Lanier,*[115] making it difficult for the appeals court to reiterate its earlier finding that Judge Lanier did not have "fair warning" that his conduct violated

[115] *Doe v. Claiborne County,* 1996 WL 734583 (12-26-96).

constitutional rights.[116] In addition, Congress has enacted legislation based on the assumption that § 242 punishes sexual assaults.[117] Finally, the U.S. Justice Department brief in *Lanier* notes that it prosecutes 30 cases per year under § 242,many based on a due process right to bodily integrity. Since 1981, the Civil Rights Division of DOJ prosecuted at least 29 §242 cases involving sexual assault by public officials, most involving a woman who was sexually assaulted by a jailer, police officer, or border patrol agent. However, three other cases besides *Lanier* involved sexual assault by state judges—two resulting in guilty pleas, the third in acquittal.

In sum, *Lanier* questioned the fundamental nature of "constitutional crimes" prohibited by § 242, a statute notable for its definitional vagueness and described by the court of appeals as "perhaps the most abstractly worded statute among the more than 700 crimes in the federal criminal code." Since the federal "rights, privileges, or immunities" whose official invasion may be the predicate for a § 242 prosecution are not plainly spelled out by statute, its scope has traditionally been determined by the courts according to contemporary constitutional understanding of those terms. Justice Souter, in his opinion, appears largely unmoved by respondent's argument that to permit a § 242 prosecution of Judge Lanier would encroach upon the traditional police powers of the state and impermissibly "federalize," by judicial decree, state offenses like rape and sexual assault into a federal "common law" of crime. Nonetheless, as noted earlier, solicitude for federalism and our dual system of government was a factor limiting Congress' commerce power to enact the Gun-Free School Zones Act in *Lopez* and could inform judicial review of the corollary issue posed by *Lanier*. To what extent, if any, such

---

[116] *See e.g. Doe v. Taylor Independent School District,* 15 F.3d 443, 451 (5th Cir.), *cert. denied,* 115 S.Ct. 70 (1994)(teacher's sexual abuse of a student "deprived [the student] of a liberty interest recognized under the substantive due process component of the Fourteenth Amendment"); *Dang Vang v. Vang Xiong X. Toyed,* 944 F.2d 476, 479 (9th Cir. 1991)(plaintiff's constitutional right were violated in a § 1983 case when she was raped by a state welfare official); and *Stoneking v. Bradford Area School District,* 882 F.2d 720, 727 (ed Cir. 1989), *cert. denied,* 493 U.S. 1044 (1990)("the constitutional right...to freedom form invasion of...personal security through sexual abuse, was well established" by the early 1980's).

[117] In the Violent Crime Control and Law Enforcement Act of 1994, Congress required enhanced punishment for several crimes in aggravated circumstances, including sexual violence. That enhancement provision applied to violations of § 242. *See* P.L. 103-322 § 320103(b)(3), 108 Stat. 2109.

objections may influence renewed judicial consideration of the case can only be speculated. At this point, however, *Lanier* appears to expand the general availability of § 242 as a safeguard against official deprivation of federal constitutional rights and, in addition, may constitutionally buttress the civil remedy for gender-motivated violence in VAWA, at least as applied to acts of violence by governmental agents or others acting under color of law.

SEXUAL HARASSMENT IN EDUCATION: RECENT LEGAL DEVELOPMENTS UNDER TITLE IX OF THE EDUCATION AMENDMENTS OF 1972

Kimberly D. Jones

The U.S. Supreme Court first recognized a claim for sexual harassment in its decision in *Meritor Savings Bank v. Vinson,* a case brought under Title VII of the Civil Rights Act of 1964 which prohibits discrimination in employment. While the Court's initial decisions dealt with sexual harassment in employment, sexual harassment claims were becoming increasingly common in the educational environment. Sexual harassment claims in education fall into three categories: sexual harassment of a student by a third person somehow affiliated with the school. Alleged victims of sexual harassment in schools have brought claims under Title IX of the Education Amendments of 1972 which prohibits discrimination based on sex on federally funded education programs and activities. In *Franklin v, Lago Vista Independent School District*, the Court held that under Title IX, a school district is not liable for sexual harassment of a student by a teacher "unless an official of the school district who at a minimum has authority to institute corrective measures on the district's behalf has actual notice of, and is deliberately indifferent to, the teacher's misconduct." The U.S. Supreme Court again addressed the issue of the liability of school districts in regard to student-on-student sexual harassment. In *Davis v. Monroe County Board of Education*, the Court held that a school district may be liable under "[a] private Title IX damages action...only where the funding recipient is deliberately indifferent to sexual harassment, of which the recipient has actual knowledge, and that harassment is so severe, pervasive, and objectively offensive that it can be said to deprive the victims of access to the educational opportunities or benefits provided by the school." Some federal courts have also considered sexual harassment committed by a third party, other than a student, who is somehow affiliated with the educational program, activity or institution. This report discusses U.S. Supreme Court decisions on the issue of sexual harassment in schools and how federal courts are addressing the issue where the questions remain. This report will be updated as needed. For further discussion of the cases summarized in this report, see CRS Report 98-727, *Title IX and School District Liability for Sexual Harassment by a Teacher:* Gebser v. Lago Vista Independent School District by Kimberly D. Jones and CRS Report RS 20211, *School District Liability for Student-on-Student Sexual Harassment*: Davis v. Monroe County Board of Education, by Kimberly D. Jones.

The U.S. Supreme Court first recognized a claim for sexual harassment in its decision in *Meritor Savings Bank v. Vinson,*[1] a case brought under Title VII of the Civil Rights Act of 1964 which prohibits discrimination in employent.[2] In *Meritor,* the Court recognized two types of sexual harassment: "harassment that involves the conditioning of concrete employment benefits of sexual favors," commonly referred to as *quid pro quo* sexual harassment "and harassment that, while not affecting economic benefits, creates a hostile or offensive working environment," commonly known as hostile environment sexual harassment.[3] In Title VII cases, the Court typically applies principles of agency to determine if an employer may be held liable for monetary damages when a supervisor sexually harasses a subordinate employee. While the Court's initial decisions dealt with sexual harassment in the educational environment where students were bringing allegations of sexual harassment by teachers or by other students under Title IX of the Education Amendments of 1972.

---

[1] 477 U.S. 57(1985). For a discussion of sexual harassment generally, see CRS Report 98-34, *Sexual Harassment and Violence Against Women: Developments in Federal Law*, by Charles V. Dale.

[2] 42 U.S.C.A. § 2000c *et seq.* (West 1994 & Supp. 1998).

[3] 477 U.S. at 62.

Title IX of the Education Amendments of 1972 states in relevant part that, "No person in the United States, shall, on the bases of sex, be excluded from participation in, be denied the benefits of, or be subjected to discrimination under any education program or activity receiving Federal financial assistance..."[4] The Office of Civil Rights within the Department of Education is charged with the administrative enforcement of Title IX. The U.S. Supreme Court has also held that an individual has an implied private right of action under Title IX to pursue a judicially imposed remedy.[5]

Since its enactment, Title IX has been primarily used by women and girls seeking equal treatment in educational programs and activities.[6] Recently, Title IX has been used as a vehicle to challenge sexual harassment in the classrooms and on campuses. In *Franklin v. Gwinnett County Public Schools*, the Court recognized a teacher's sexual harassment of a student as a form of discrimination based on sex that violated Title IX and allowed the victim to receive monetary damages.[7] However, the *Franklin* decision did not address the question of when a school district would be liable for monetary damages for the sexual harassment of a student by a district teacher. Nor did the *Franklin* decision address the district's liability for sexual harassment f a student by another student. This report summarizes the recent legal development sin the area of Title IX and sexual harassment since the Court's decision in *Franklin.*

SEXUAL HARASSMENT OF A STUDENT BY TEACHER

In *Gebser v. Lago Vista Independent School District*,[8] the Court established the standard of liability that courts apply when determining if a school district should be held liable for monetary damages under Title IX when a district teacher sexually harasses a student. In *Gebser*, a high school teacher entered into a sexual relationship with one of his students. The

[4] 20 U.S.C.A. §1681 (West 1990 & Supp. 1998).

[5] Cannon v. University of Chicago, 441 U.S. 677 (1979).

[6] Cohen v. Brown University, 101 F.3d 155 (1st Cir. 1996), *cert. denied,* 520 U.S. 1186 (1977).

[7] 503 U.S. 60 (1992).

[8] 524 U.S. 274, 118 S. Ct. 1989 (1998). See also CRS Report RS20211, *Title IX and School District Liability for Sexual Harassment by a Teacher:* Gebser v. Lago Vista Independent School District, by Kimberly D. Jones.

relationship continued with the two often having sexual intercourse during class time, but not on school property. The student never informed school officials or her parents about the relationship. The relationship was brought to light after they were discovered by police. The teacher was criminally prosecuted, fired from his teaching position, and had his teaching license revoked by the state. The Court held that liability for monetary damages under Title IX will not lie "unless an official of the school district who at a minimum has authority to institute corrective measures on the district's behalf has actual notice of, and is deliberately indifferent to, the teacher's misconduct."[9] Since no appropriate official of the school district was even aware of the relationship, let alone able to take corrective measures, the student was unable to recover monetary damages.

SEXUAL HARASSMENT OF STUDENT BY ANOTHER STUDENT

The issue of when a school district will be held liable for sexual harassment of a student committed by another student or students was addressed by the U.S. Supreme Court in *Davis v. Monroe County Board of Education.*[10] Aurelia Davis brought suit, on behalf of her daughter LaShonda, against the Monroe County Board of Education and two school officials alleging violation of Title IX for their failure to prevent a fellow student from sexually harassing LaShonda.[11] Davis' suit sought $500,000 in compensatory and punitive damages. The Davis' complaint was dismissed by the district court, but on appeal was reinstated by a three judge panel of the 11th Circuit. The school board sought a rehearing of the decision before the full panel of the 11th Circuit, which reversed the three-judge panel and dismissed Davis'

---

[9] 118 S. Ct. at 1993.

[10] 120 F.3d 1390 (11th Cir. 1997), *rev'd,*__U.S.__.No. 97-843, slip op. (U.S. May 24, 1999).

[11] LaShonda Davis alleges that during her 5th grade year at Hubbard Elementary School she was subjected to at least eight incidents of sexual harassment committed by a male student who was in several of her classes. She allegedly reported these incidents to three of her teachers, to the school's principal and to her mother. In addition, Aurelia Davis, complained to the school principal and to two teachers about the incidents. The harassment stopped when the male student was charged with sexual battery. Davis alleged that LaShonda's grades dropped and she threatened suicide because of the harassing behavior.

Title IX claim. Davis appealed to the U.S. Supreme Court which agreed to hear the appeal.[12]

On appeal, the Supreme Court reversed the decision of the 11th Circuit Court of Appeals, finding that a school district, under certain circumstances, may be liable under Title IX for student-on-student sexual harassment. Justice O'Connor, writing for the majority, held that "[a]private Title IX damages action may lie against a school board in cases of student-on-student harassment, but only where the funding recipient is deliberately indifferent to sexual harassment, of which the recipient has actual knowledge, and that harassment is so severe, pervasive, and objectively offensive that it can be said to deprive the victims of access to the educational opportunities or benefits provided by the school."[13]

In this case, the harassment took place "during school hours and on school grounds."[14] The majority then concluded "that recipients of federal funding may be liable for 'subject[ing]' their students to discrimination where the recipient is deliberately indifferent to known acts of student-on-student sexual harassment and the harasser is under the school's disciplinary authority."[15] According to Justice O'Connor, the "deliberate indifference" standard "sought to eliminate any 'risk that the recipient would be liable in damages not for its own official decision but instead for its employees' independent actions.'"[16]

The *Davis* decision also provided guidance on what is actionable for discrimination under Title IX. Justice O'Connor defined discrimination under Title IX as sexual harassment that is "so severe, pervasive and objectively offensive that it can be said to deprive the victims to access to the educational opportunities or benefits provided by the school."[17] The majority further defined discrimination as "behavior...serious enough to have the systemic effect of denying the victim equal access to an education program or activity."[18] Some factors the Court found compelling were "the ages of the harasser and the victim and the number of individuals involved."[19] the Court

---

[12] 120 F.3d 1390 (11th Cir. 1997), *cert. granted in part*, 66 U.S.L.W. 3387 (U.S. Sept 29, 1998) (No. 97-843).
[13] No. 97-843, slip op. at 1 (U.S. May 24, 1999).
[14] No. 97-843, slip op. at 15.
[15] *Id.* at 16.
[16] *Id.* at 11 (quoting Gebser v. Lago Vista Indep. Sch. Dist., 524 U.S. 274, 290-291).
[17] *Id. at 19-20.*
[18] *Id.* at 22.
[19] *Id.* at 20.

explicitly noted that "[d]amages are not available for simple acts of teasing and name-calling among school children...even where these comments target differences in gender."[20]

The Court's holding stressed that it is not meant to dictate the type of discipline that schools must use and urges lower courts to "refrain from second guessing the disciplinary decisions made by school administrators."[21] To ensure this, the majority stated that the decision of school administrators will bet be disturbed unless their "response to the harassment or lack thereof is clearly unreasonable in light of the known circumstances."[22] The Court noted that "[A] university might not, for example, be expected to exercise the same degree of control over its students that a grade school
would enjoy...and it would enjoy...and it would be reasonable for a school to refrain from a form of disciplinary action that would expose it to constitutional or statutory claims."[23]

The decision reinstated Davis' Title IX claim on the ground that she may be able to meet the above standard based on her allegations of "repeated acts of sexual harassment," multiple victims, and the "negative effect on her daughter's ability to receive an education."[24] The Court also noted that there was support for the conclusion that G.F.'s actions were severe, pervasive, and objectionably offensive, and that Davis warranted an opportunity to "show both actual knowledge and deliberate indifference on the part of the Board, which made no effort whatsoever either to investigate or to put an end of the harassment."[25]

Sexual Harassment of Student by Third Party

While claims alleging sexual harassment by a teacher or fellow student are more common, at least one federal court has considered sexual harassment committed by a third party who is somehow affiliated with the educational program, activity or institution. In *brown v. Hot, Sexy and Safer Productions,*

[20] *id.* at 21.
[21] *Id.* at 17.
[22] *Id.*
[23] *id.* at 23.
[24] *Id.* at 23.
[25] *Id.* at 23.

Inc., two students and their parents brought a hostile environment sexual harassment claim under Title IX based on an AIDS awareness program put on by the school, but conducted by an individual contracted by the school."[26] The students alleged that the presenter's profane, offensive, and sexually oriented language created a hostile sexual environment. The court, noting the dearth of Title IX caselaw in the area, referred to Title VII caselaw to analyze the case.[27] The court relied on the same Title VII elements that the 10th Circuit Court of Appeals use in the Seamon v. Snow.[28] There, the court held that for a school to be held liable for hostile environment sexual harassment, the plaintiff must show:

(1) that he is a member of a protected group;
(2) that he was subject to unwelcome harassment;
(3) that the harassment was based on sex;
(4) that the sexual harassment was sufficiently severe or pervasive so as unreasonably to alter the conditions of his education and create an abusive educational environment, and
(5) that some basis for institutional liability has been established.[29]

The court concluded that the students had failed to state a claim under Title IX based on these factors.

[26] 68 F.3d 525 (1st Cir. 1995), *cert. denied, 516 U.S. 1159 (1996).*

[27] 68 F.3d at 540. "Because the relevant caselaw under title IX is relatively sparse, we apply Title VII caselaw by analogy."

[28] 84 F.3d 1126 (10th Cir. 1996).

[29] 84 F.3d at 1232.

SEXUAL HARASSMENT IN THE WORKPLACE: SELECTED REFERENCES

Jean Bowers

I. DEFINITION OF ISSUES AND TRENDS

Burstein, James A.
Sexual harassment's second generation: the harasser as 'victim'.
Employee relations law journal, v. 21. No. 2, Sept 22, 1995: 153
LRS95-1408

"Employers confronted with complaints of workplace sexual harassment have become increasingly aggressive in addressing these claims. While doing so may prevent litigation by the complaining employee, such response can give rise to legal claims from the accused....Employee 'victims' thinking themselves wrongfully disciplined for harassment have challenged the discipline on various grounds, alleging (1) contractual claims, (2) defamation, (3) employment discrimination, (4) negligence, (5) intentional infliction of emotional distress, and (6) breach of public policy."

Charney, Dara A. Russell, Ruth C.

An overview of sexual harassment. American journal of psychiatry, v. 151, Jan. 1994: 10-17.

LRS94-7540

"Computerized literature searches were used to identify research and review papers from psychiatry and psychology journals. Nonscientific works that provide additional information are also cited. The literature suggests that sexual harassment is a widespread phenomenon, affecting 42% of women and 15% of men in occupational settings, 73% of women and 22% of men during medical training, and lower percentages in other educational settings. Despite the pervasive nature of this problem, only 1%-7% of victims file formal complaints. Sexual harassment produces an array of psychological and physical symptoms in over 90% of victims, and 12% seek help from mental health care professionals."

Crawford, Susan.

Economic impact of sexual harassment in the workplace. USA today (magazine), v. 123, Mar. 1995: 35

LRS95-14809

"To date, there is only limited research that quantifies the dollar costs of sexual harassment. The data that does exist is compelling, however. In the typical Fortune 500 company with 23,750 employees, sexual harassment costs $6,700,00 per year in absenteeism, low productivity, and employee turnover. This represents $282.53 per employee, according to a 1988 survey conducted by Working Woman. (The first scientific sampling of its kind in the private sector, this 49-question survey was answered by directors of personnel, human resources, and equal-opportunity offices representing 3,300,00 employees at 160 corporations.)"

Debating sexual correctness: pornography, sexual harassment, date rape and the politics of sexual equality. Edited by Adele M. Stan. New York, Delta, c1995. 286 p. HQ1237.5U6 D43 1995

Partial contents.—Flashpoints: the Meese Commission, Tailhook, Hill-Thomas, and the Antioch sex code.—Rights and wrongs in the intimate arena.—Sex war in the media.—When the personal becomes political.—The Dworkin-MacKinnon Antipornography Civil Rights Ordinance (Minneapolis).—Selected results from the Ms. Magazine Campus Project on Sexual Assault.

Feliu, Alfred G. Fealy. Elizabeth A.

The role of "sex" in same-sex harassment claims. Employee relations law journal, v. 21, spring 1996: 39-60.

"This article focuses on the proper meaning and scope of the term 'sex' under Title VII. It reviews the rapidly developing case law in the area of same-sex sexual harassment and the arguments for and against recognizing such a cause of action under Title VII. Finally, this article attempts to answer the two crucial and determinative questions in this area, namely, whether 'sex' as that term is employed in Title VII encompasses same-sex sexual harassment claims and, if so, what burden of proof must be met to establish such a claim. This article concludes that same-sex sexual harassment claims are actionable under Title VII but only under very limited circumstances, namely, where an anti-male or anti-female atmosphere is shown to exist."

Gates, David.

White male paranoia. Newsweek, v. 121, Mar. 29, 1993: 48-54.

LRS93-1374

Men in the 90s have become victims too.

Glazer, Sarah.

Crackdown on sexual harassment: is the nation overreacting to the problem? CQ researcher, v. 6, July 19, 1996: whole issue (625-648 p.).

LRS96-4317

"The nation's sensitivity to sexual harassment has changed profoundly since October 1991, when Anita Hill's harassment charges against Supreme Court nominee Clarence Thomas riveted Americans to their TV sets. Sexual harassment claims filed with the federal government have increased dramatically, as have damages paid to successful plaintiffs. Some critics sympathetic to business say the nation has overreacted. They attack several recent multimillion-dollar jury awards as excessive punishments for what they claim is nothing more than crude sexual joking at work. Women's-rights activists respond that sexual harassment is often emotionally devastating, and that only a tiny proportion of the women who have been harassed ever file formal complaints, though harassment is a widespread problem in the workplace."

Hebert, L. Camille.

Sexual harassment is gender harassment. University of Kansas law review, v. 43, Apr. 1995: 556-607.

LRS95-6224

Concludes that "the separate treatment of and the application of different standards for sexual harassment and gender harassment by the EEOC is not justified by any differences between the types of employer action described in the two sets of EEOC guidelines. The EEOC should recognize that both sexual conduct and nonsexual conduct is used to denigrate or show hostility toward women in the context of the workplace, and that, therefore, what is labeled sexual harassment and what is labeled gender harassment are really the same type of discriminatory conduct."

Holcombe, B.J. (Barbara Jean) Wellington, Charmaine.

Search for justice: a woman's path to renewed self-esteem from the fear, shame, and anger of sexual harassment and employment discrimination. Walpole, NH, Stillpoint Pub., c1992. 225 p.

HD6060.5.U5H65 1992

"Sexual harassment and employment discrimination are a social injustice that blights the lives of talented, dedicated women. They frustrate achievements, thwart purpose and undermine morale of bright, ambitious individuals willing to offer their talents to society. So this social injustice, like a disease, saps the vitality from our society." Includes sexual harassment scenarios.

King, Chad W.

Sex, love letters, and vicious rumors: anticipating new situations creating sexually hostile work environments. BYU journal of public law, v. 9, no. 2, 1995: 341-365.

LES95-7421

Comment examines the expanding legal definition of what may constitute sexual harassment in the workplace, including unchecked rumors about one's personal life and unwanted love letters. "In light of the lack of consensus in the courts in defining harassment, employers should take a conservative view of sexually hostile work environment harassment and develop aggressive, thorough policies and definitions."

McCann, Nancy Dodd. McGinn, Thomas A.

Harassed: 100 women define inappropriate behavior in the workplace. Homewood, Ill., Business One Irwin, c1992. 128 p.

HD6060.3.M33 1992

Partial contents.—"Reasonable women" define harassment.—The "reasonable woman" standard.—How the law has developed.—Current sexual harassment laws: defined and explained.—The real costs of discrimination.—The effects of harassment and discrimination.—The challenge of changing the workplace—Meeting the challenge with programs and training.

McNerney, Donald J.

New legal worry: third-party sexual harassment. HRfocus, v. 73, July 1996: 1, 4-6.

LRS96-5808

"Companies face a new set of liabilities. Not only do they have to protect employees from unwelcome sexual advances from coworkers, but they also have to protect then form unwelcome advances from third parties—customers, clients, vendors, contingent workers, members of the general public and the like."

Ness, Beverly J.

The road to respect which a reasonable woman must travel: sexual harassment in the American workplace. Federal Bar news & journal, v. 40, June 1993: 280-287.

Examines sexual harassment by focusing on its historic background, early cases, the development of the hostile environment standard, the Supreme Court decision in Meritor Savings Bank, FSB v. Vinson, and important characteristics of sexual harassment at work.

Sexual correctness. Newsweek, v. 122, Oct. 25, 1993: 52-58, 61-62, 64.
LRS93-9594

Contents.—Sexual correctness: has it gone too far? By Sarah Crichton.—Abused and confused, by Michele Ingrassia.—Whose hype? By Susal Faludi.—Stop whining, by Mary Matalin.—Balancing act, by Susan Estrich.

Skaine, Rosemarie.

Power and gender: issues in sexual dominance and harassment.

Jefferson, N.C., McFarland & Co., c1996. 460 p.

HQ1237.5U6 S53 1996

Contents.—Defining sexual harassment.—The history of sexual harassment in America.—Theoretical framework.—Legal dimensions.—Incidence and settings.—Victims and harassers.—Sexual harassment in government.—Sexual harassment in education.—Sexual harassment in the military.—Strategies for the victim.—Policy strategies for the organization and society.—A society without sexual harassment.

Stop sexual harassment [Online}. Available Internet:

http//www,resources/org:80/web.html (as of Jan. 21, 1997)

Contents.—Internet resources.—Definition.—A resource list (State-by-State resources, National-level resources, Other women's groups, Resources on the Internet).—What to do.—The law.

Reference material on the Internet for which CRS is providing an address only.

II. Prevention and Remedial Action

Brandenburg, Judith Berman.

Sexual harassment: a challenge to schools of education. Washington, American Association of Colleges for Teacher Education, c1995, 31 p.

LC212.862.B73 1995

As the problem of sexual harassment becomes more visible, many institutions are requesting advice. This monograph seeks to assist schools of education to develop effective policies, procedures, and environments that prohibit sexual harassment and to prepare professionals who will understand the issue and will be equipped to prevent its occurrence. A major focus is sexual harassment involving student teachers during field-based practice teaching.

Englander, Jeffrey P.

Handling sexual harassment in the workplace. CPA journal, v. 62, Feb. 1992: 14, 16-18, 20-22.

LRS92-1035

"Pubic consciousness has been sparked once again and a course of action by every employer is clearly needed! The author presents a background of both federal and state legislation and instances of careless and even unintended violations resulting in sanctions, fines and other adverse consequences. Here also is a series of thoughtful steps an employer can take to set the appropriate environment for employees."

Goodson, Jane. Lewis, Christine. Culverhouse, Renee.

The tort of outrage: how sexual harassment have been pursued under Title VII of the Civil Rights Act of 1964. But by using workers' compensation and the tort of intentional infliction of emotional distress, victims are forging a new strategy."

Hallinan. Kathleen M.

Invasion of privacy or protection against sexual harassment: co-employee dating and employer liability. Columbia journal of law and social problems, v. 26, spring 1993: 435-464.

LRS93-6727

Comment "analyzes cases in which courts have addressed the relationship between employer regulation of co-employee dating and the law governing sexual harassment. The Author concludes that employers should implement specific policies on co-employee dating, including a prohibition on dating between supervisors and their direct subordinates."

Hauck, Vern E. Pearce, Thomas G.

Sexual harassment and arbitration. Labor law journal, v. 43, Jan. 1992: 31-39.

LRS92-2178

Article provides "insight into how labor arbitrators are currently dealing with sexual harassment grievances. The results of an in-depth analysis of one hundred published labor arbitration awards are reported."

Lightle, Juliana. Doucet, Elizabeth H.

Sexual harassment in the workplace: a guide to prevention. Los Altos, Calif., Crisp Publications, c1992. 116 p. (Fifty-Minute series)

KF3467.Z9L54 1992

Contents.—What is sexual harassment?—EEOC guidelines and sexual harassment.—Preventing sexual harassment in the workplace.—Handling sexual harassment complaints.—Governmental agencies and the courts.—Maintaining a positive work environment.—Solutions to case studies and questions.

Lindemann, Barbara. Kadue, David D.

Sexual harassment in employment day. Washington, Bureau of National Affairs, c1992. 824 p.

KF3467.L56 1992

Contents.—Theories of liability under Title VII.—Other sources of legal protection.—Preventive, investigative, and remedial action.—Special litigation issues.

Lynch, Frances.

Draw the line: a sexual harassment-free workplace. 1s ed. Grants Pass, OR., Oasis Press/PSI Research, c1995. 150 p. (PSI successful business library)

HF5549.5.S45L95 1995

"Designed to help you understand what legally qualifies as sexual harassment in today's courts and to guide your efforts to create a harassment-free workplace."

Naylor, Greg A.

HF5549.5S45n39 1996

M.Lee Smith, c1996. 82 p.

Partial contents.—Employer liability.—Protecting your organization against harassment liability.—Defenses against harassment actions.—Remedies and administrative requirements.—Internal company sex harassment policies.—No dating/no fraternization policies.—For men only.—For women only.

Niven, Daniel.

The case of the hidden harassment. Harvard business review, v. 70, Mar.-Apr. 1992: 12-14, 16-17, 20, 22-23.

LRS92-2686

"What happens when a manager's responsibilities clash with an employee's right to privacy? Five experts on sexual harassment in the workplace examine his options."

Oh, James J.

Internal sexual harassment complaints: investigating to win. Employee relations law journal, v. 18, autumn 1992: 227-244.

LRS92-7469

"In a sexual harassment lawsuit, a company has a unique opportunity to avoid liability if it can prove that, when the sexual harassment complaint arose internally, the company promptly investigated the complaint and implemented corrective action to prevent the harassment from occurring again. This is a how-to-article; how to investigate a complaint of sexual harassment in order to limit or even eliminate the company's liability in a lawsuit brought either by the alleged victim or alleged perpetrator of the sexual harassment."

Powell, Elizabeth.

Sex on your terms: what to say—to explain your limits, to repel sexual pressure, to avoid being falsely accused, to escape disease. Boston, MA, Allyn & Bacon, 1996. 238 p.

HQ23.P69 1996

Tamminen, Julie M.

Sexual harassment in the workplace: managing corporate policy. New York, Wiley, c1994. 543 p. (Human resources library)

KF3467.T36 1994

Contents.—Managerial and legal challenges in preventing sexual harassment.—Drafting a preventive sexual harassment policy.—Sexual harassment complaint procedure.—Sexual harassment resolution.—Administration of the preventive policy.—Sexual harassment training.—Handling charges of sexual harassment.—Current discovery issues in sexual harassment claims.

Woldt, Wendy A.

Sexual harassment in the workplace: a practical guide for employers. Berkeley, CA, Continuing Education of the Bar, California, 1995. 58 p.

KFC573.W65W65 1995

Partial contents.—Policies and procedures to minimize sexual harassment.—Reporting, investigative, and disciplinary procedures.—Legal remedies for sexual harassment.

III. Sectors of Concern

A. Politics and Government

Beaupre, Laurier W.

Birth of a third immunity? President Bill Clinton secures temporary immunity from trial. Boston College law review, 36, July 1995: 725-767.

LRS95-12843

Comment disagrees with the 1994 federal district court holding that "a sitting President [is] entitled to absolute temporary immunity from civil damages suits based on actions that occurred before he took office." The author argues that this decision, made in the Paula Jones sexual harassment case against President Clinton, should be replaced "with a doctrine of presumptive amenability to suit."

Gender, race, and the politics of Supreme Court appointments: the import of the Anita Hill/Clarence Thomas hearings. Southern California law review, v. 65, Mar. 1992: 1279-1582

LRS92-4335

Presents articles and comments in three sections: Sexual Harassment: Myths, Literature, and Law (Martha R. Mahoney, Amy Richlin, Judith Resnik, Hilary M. Schor, Tania Modelski, Charles R. Lawrence III, Estelle B. Freedman, Adrienne D. Davis and Stephanie M. Wildman, Susan Estrich, Louise F. Fitzgerald, Carol Sanger, Christine A. Littleton, Stephen Reinhardt, and Abby J. Leibman); Anita Hill One Month Later: Remarks Before the National Forum for Women State Legislators (Anita Hill spoke at this conference held in San Diego on Nov. 15, 1991,followed by Susan Deller Ross, Deborah L. Rhode, and Kimberle Crenshaw); and The View from and to Congress (Ronald R. Garet, Erwin Chemerinksy, David B. Wilkins, Dennis E. Curtis, Christopher H. Schroeder, Carolyn G. Heilbrun, and Glenn Harlan Reynolds.)

Gladstone. Leslie W.

Sexual harassment policy: rules applicable to congressional offices. Revised Jan. 21, 1997. Washington, Congressional Research Service, 1997. 4p.

97-135 GOV

Policy on sexual harassment in congressional offices is governed by P.L. 104-1,the Congressional Accountability Act of 1995, that applies 11 civil rights and labor laws to the legislative branch of the federal government. One of the statutes applied, Title VII of the Civil Rights Act of 1964, has been interpreted by the Supreme Court to forbid sexual harassment.

Gordon, Dianna.

It's not about sex—it's about power. State legislatures, v. 19, 1993: 51, 53, 55, 57.

LRS93-6142

Describes what steps state legislatures have taken to handle instances of sexual harassment among legislators.

Kaufman, Leslie.

Sexual harassment. Government executive, v. 74, Apr. 1992: 42-45.

LRS92-2087

Examines personnel practices in federal agencies in response to the growing awareness of sexual harassment. "The government is responding with stepped-up training and streamlined complaint procedures."

Manley, Will.

Sexual harassment by patrons. Part 1-4. American libraries, v. 24, Jan., July, Sept., Oct. 1993: 1-10.

LRS93-12512

"Although I had a sense that sexual harassment by patrons has always been a problem for working librarians, I had no idea how severe and widespread that problem is until the responses to my survey came back. Not only did 1,816 women indicate that they had been harassed, but almost 35% of that group felt so strongly about their experience that they made unsolicited comments on the subject."

McCormack, William U.

Managing relations between the sexes in a law enforcement organization. FBI law enforcement bulletin, v. 64, Jan. 1995: 27-32.

LRS95-908

"Police managers responsible for fostering a workplace free of sexual intimidation and hostility may be justified in imposing reasonable restrictions on superior/subordinate relationships when necessary."

Morin, Richard.

Female aides on Hill: still outsiders in man's world. Washington Post, Feb 21, 1993: A1, A18-A19.

LRS93-909

Present results of a Jan. 1993 survey of 603 female and 200 male congressional employees. "They talked about a still-dominant male culture on [Capitol] Hill that made even senior female staff workers feel like 'outsiders'—and sometimes like intruders...Sexual harassment on the job is as prevalent in Congress as it is in work places across the country, according to Post surveys."

Politic, values, and the Thomas nomination. PS: political science and politics, v. 25, Sept. 1992: 473-495.

LRS92-7823

Contents.—The Thomas appointment; defeats and victories for women, by Marian Lief Palley and Howard A. Palley.—Senate process, congressional politics, ant the Thomas nomination, by Barbara Sinclair.—Public opinion and the Thomas nomination, by Kathleen Frankovic and Joyce Gelb.—Divisions in the civil rights community, by Dianne M. Pinderhughes.—Race trumps gender: the Thomas nomination in the Black community, by Jane Mansbridge and Katherine Tate.—The effects of the Thomas appointment to the Supreme Court, by Karen O'Connor.

Rosen, Jeffrey.

One bite at the apple. New Republic, v. 216, Feb. 3, 1997: 14., 16-17.

LRS97-72

"At the Supreme Court arguments on Monday, January 13, in Clinton v. Jones, the justices seemed inclined to delay Paula Jones's sexual harassment suit until the president leaves office, because the president is a busy man. But even if President Clinton is temporarily spared the mortifying task of answering Jones's complaint, his trial in the court of popular opinion has already begun. In the wake of an article by Stuart Taylor in The American Lawyer [LRS96-8738], there is a growing consensus that not only are Paula Jones's allegations true, but that they also amount to a clear case of legally actionable sexual harassment—a 'far more serious' case, Taylor argues, than Anita Hill's accusations against Clarence Thomas."

Sharpe, Rochelle.

Capitol Hill's worst kept secret: sexual harassment. Ms., v. 2, Jan.-Feb. 1992: 28-45.

LRS92-451

Includes: The nature of the beast, by Anita Hill.—Refusing to be silenced: the bread and circus literacy test, by Patricia J. Williams.—"Ain't gonna let nobody turn me around," by Barbara Smith.—Becoming the third wave, by Rebecca Walker.—We speak in tongues, by Marcia Ann Gillespie.--...And the language is race, by Eleanor Holmes Norton.

Straight, Michael.

Accountability for racial, religious, ethnic and gender bias misconduct and sexual harassment by federal judges. In U.S. National Commission on Judicial Discipline and Removal. Research papers. Vol.2. Washington, The Commission, 1993. P. 1679-1786.

LRS93-10675

"This report explores the mechanisms that can be used to achieve accountability for these various types of bias misconduct, particularly in light of the understandable reluctance of some victims to complain formally about such misconduct."

Taylor, Stuart, Jr.

Her case against Clinton. American lawyer, Nov. 18996:57.

LRS96-8738

"Millions of Clinton supporters still disdain Clarence Thomas as a sexual harasser. But a comparison of the Paula Jones and Anita Hill episodes suggests that the evidence against the president is far stronger than the media has let on—and far stronger than the evidence against Thomas."

Thacker, Rebecca A. Gohmann, Stephen F.

Male/female differences in perceptions and effects of hostile environment sexual harassment: "reasonable" assumptions? Public personnel management, v. 22, Sept. 22, 1993: 1-10.

LRS93-12511

"The purpose of this paper is to explore, first of all, the notion that gender-based differences in interpretation of sexually harassing behaviors do, in fact, exist. Secondly, the paper explores the notion that the reasonable person standard may also be too broad for determining the effects of hostile work environment harassment, and that the psychological and emotional effects of hostile work environment harassment will also differ systematically by gender. Data from a major survey of sexual harassment among public employees in the Federal workplace are analyzed, and implications for organizational policy are discussed."

U.S. Congress. Senate. Committee on Veterans' Affairs.

VA health-care programs for women veterans. Hearings, 102nd Congress, 2nd session. June 30 and July 2, 1992. Washington, G.P.O., 1992. 476 p. (Hearing, Senate, 102nd Congress, 2nd session, S. Hrg. 102-922)

KF26.V4 1992a

Contents.—The counseling and other needs of women veterans who were sexually assaulted or harassed while active duty and VA's ability to respond.—Legislation regarding VA health-care for women veterans (S.2028) and oversight of VA health-care programs for women veterans, including women veterans who were sexually assaulted or harassed during military service.

U.S. Merit Systems Protection Board. Office of Policy and Evaluation.

Sexual harassment in the federal workplace: trends, progress, continuing challenges. Washington, The Board, G.P.O., 1995. 73 p.

JK850.S45U55 1995

"This report discusses the results of a study undertaken by the Board to determine the nature and extent of sexual harassment in the Federal Government. It updates the findings of our 1980 and 1987 [JK721.U57 1981] studies on this issue. The results of the current study indicate that unwanted sexual attention remains a widespread problem in the Federal sector. At the same time, however, federal agencies have made strides in educating their workforces and raising the level of sensitivity to the issues surrounding sexual harassment."

B. Military

Barto, William T.

Sexual harassment and the Uniform Code of Military Justice: a primer for the military justice practitioner. Army lawyer, no. 272, July 1995: 3-16.

LRS95-6790

"After an introductory consideration of the criminal aspects of sexual harassment under the UCMJ, the article surveys the legal issues that may emerge when prosecuting sexual harassment—either as cruelty and maltreatment in violation of Article 93, UCMJ, or when charged as a violation of one or more of the remaining punitive articles. The article concludes with a summary of the substantive law in this area and provides recommendations for the military justice practitioner."

Chema, J. Richard

Arresting "Tailhook": the prosecution of sexual harassment in the military. Military law review, v. 140, spring 1993: 1-64.

LRS93-10184

"Examines conduct that commonly is referred to a sexual harassment and discusses how it can be prosecuted under current provisions of the UCMJ."

Equal opportunity. Prepared by the American Forces Information Service. [Washington?] Current News Analysis & Research Service, 1992. 51 p. (U.S. Dept. of Defense. Current news, special edition, no. 1911 (June 1992)

LRS92-5329

A collection of newspaper articles addressing questions of Blacks, women, ang garys in the military.

Gleick, Elizabeth.

Scandal in the military. Time, Nov. 25, 1996: 28.

LRS96-8752

The army "announced it was filing rape, assault and sexual harassment charges against three male officers responsible for training new recruits at Aberdeen [Proving Ground], and investigating at least 17 others. The most far-reaching scandal to hit the armed forces since the Navy's 1991 Tailhook incident."

Gruenwald, Juliana.

Army defends record on sex harassment. Congressional Quarterly weekly report, v. 55, Feb. 8, 1997: 376.

LRS97-362

"Generals vow to ensure women's safety in coeducational training."

Laurent, Anne.

Unfriendly fire. Advocate, no. 615, Nov 3, 1992: 50-52.

LRS92-9624

"The Pentagon ban on gays in the armed forces is coercing lesbians to be silent about sexual harassment."

Luddy, John.

"Tailhook" aftermath: don't feminize the fleet. Washington, Heritage Foundation, 1992. 3 p. (Backgrounder no. 184)

LRS92-5018

This Heritage Foundation backgrounder updates another Heritage study on the issue of women in combat. "As Navy, Congress, and the American people consider the now notorious 'Tailhook' sexual misconduct case, perspective is required."

McMichael, William H.

The mother of all hooks: the story of the U.S. Navy's Tailhook Scandal. New Brunwick, NJ, Transaction Publishers, 1997. VB324.W65M38 1997 Projected publication date: 9701

U.S. General Accounting Office.

DOD service academies: update on extent of sexual harassment; report to congressional requesters. Mar. 31, 1995. Washington, G.A.O., 1995. 34 p.

LRS95-2599

"GAO/NSIAD-95-58, B-259415"

Updates an earlier GAO study on the topic. Compares 1990-91 data with 1993-94 data.

C. Private Industry

Association of the Bar of the City of New York. Committee on Labor and Employment Law.

Law firm policies on workplace sexual harassment. Record of the Association of the Bar of the City of New York, v. 48, Mar. 1993: 179-193.

LRS93-10695

"This [article] explains the importance to law firms of aggressively implementing a sexual harassment policy and recommends the adoption of a model policy [Appendix A] for its prevention. The model policy includes an explanation of sexual harassment and a complaint procedure, along with a description of the steps to be taken in investigating and remedying harassment claims."

Esters, Stephanie D.

Sex-harassment policies seen needed in hospitals. National underwriter, v. 100, Sept 20, 1996: 9, 22.

LRS96-8778

"America's hospitals and healthcare facilities are not immune from the sexual harassment claims afflicting other organizations."

Iwao, Sumiko.

Women: sexual harassment I. [San Francisco] Asia Foundation, 1992. 5 p.

LRS92-8494

"Almost 10 percent of American women employed in U.S. subsidiaries of Japanese companies complained of sexual harassment, according to research."

Sexual harassment & discrimination in the workplace. Houston, Tex., Nu-Tec Pub., c1990- Vol. 1, no. 1 (July 1990)-Frequency: Monthly

Special issue: women in business. Business horizons, v. 36,Mar.-Apr. 1993: whole issue (90 p.)

LRS93-2296

Partial contents.—Cracks in the glass: the silent competence of women, by Dan R. Dalton and Idalene F. Kesner.—Attitudes toward women as managers: still the same, by Crystal L. Owen and William D. Todor.—Sex stereotyping in the workplace: a manager's guide by Eileen P. Kelly et al.—Harassment in the 1990s, by Terry Morehead Dworkin.—Female entrepreneurs: how far have they come?, by E. Holly Buttner.—Women on the move in family business, by Patricia A. Frishkoff and Bonnie M. Brown.—American female expatriates and the Civil Rights Act of 1991: balancing legal and business interests, by Patricia Feltes, Robert K. Robinson, and Ross L. Fink.

U.S. Congress. House. Committee on Education and Labor. Subcommittee on Employment Opportunities.

Hearing on sexual harassment in nontraditional occupations. Hearing, 102nd Congress, 2nd session. June 25, 1992. Washington, G.P.O., 1992. 517 p.

KF27.E3366 1992a.

"Serial no. 102-117"

The hearing focused "on sexual harassment and other forms of gender discrimination suffered by women working in traditionally male occupations such as the skilled trades and the fields of science and engineering."

Weaver, Carolyn.

A secret no more. Washington journalism review, v. 14, Sept. 1992: 23-27.

LRS92-776

"At long last, the press is struggling to confront its own sexual harassment problem. But much remains hidden confidential settlements."

D. Education

Carroll, Constance M.

Sexual harassment on campus: enhancing awareness and promoting change. Educational record, v. 74, winter 1993: 21-26.

LRS93-2649

"Through affirmative efforts and attention to preventive measures, colleges and universities can become models of humane and professional standards of interaction at all levels."

Coleman, Arthur L. Alger, Jonathan R.

Beyond speech codes: harmonizing rights of free speech and freedom from discrimination on university campuses. Journal of college and university law, v. 23, summer 1996: 91-132.

"This article argues that college and university speech codes that define prohibited behaviors abstractly, and that broadly distinguish between protected speech and regulable conduct, are likely to be successfully challenged in court." The authors recommend that colleges "promulgate policies that track anti-discrimination laws and explicitly recognize the different types of opportunities and benefits at stake in different educational contexts," that they "articulate values of tolerance and civility, and respond with 'more speech' when racist or sexist expression takes place," and that administrators use "content-neutral regulations to limit disruptive behavior and expression."

Hostile hallways: the AAUW survey on sexual harassment in America's schools. S.1., Harris/Scholastic Research, 1993. 25 p. (Study number 923012)

LRS93-11908

"The questions we wanted answered: How widespread is sexual harassment in school? Who is doing it...and to whom? Where is it happening? What forms does it take? How are kids affected by it—what happens to their attitudes toward school and their ability to learn, grow, and achieve?"

Saltzman, Amy.

It's not just teasing. U.S. news & world report, v. 115, Dec 6, 1993: 73-77.

LRS93-11144

"Sexual harassment starts young. Here's how some schools discourage it."

Sexual harassment in medical training. New England journal of medicine, v. 328, Feb. 4, 1993: 322-326.

LRS93-560

Surveys returned by 82 out of 133 internal medicine residents found that twenty-four women (73 percent) and 11 men (22 percent) reported that they had been sexually harassed at least once during either medical school or residency, although only two women had reported the harassment.

Sherer, Monica L.

No longer just child's play: school liability under Title IX for peer sexual harassment. University of Pennsylvania law review, v. 141, May 1993: 2119-2168.

LRS93-3658

Comment holds "that student-to-student sexual harassment is a legitimate and pervasive problem in elementary and secondary schools...Because schools frequently ignore, trivialize, or condone peer sexual harassment complaints, and because adequate state sexual harassment remedies often do not exist, this Comment advocates that title IX should provide a student an avenue for redress."

Special issue: violence and youth. Harvard educational review, v. 65, summer 1995: whole issue (127-366 p.)

LRS95-4818

Partial contents.—Sexual harassment in school: the public performance of gendered violence.—Reconstructing masculinity in the locker room: the mentors in violence prevention project.—Cultivating a morality of care in African American adolescents: a culture-based model of violence prevention.—Preventing and producing violence: a critical analysis of responses to school violence.—Life after death: critical pedagogy in an urban classroom.

Stein, Nan. Marshall, Nancy L. Tropp, Linda R.

Secrets in public: sexual harassment in our schools; a report on the results of a Seventeen magazine survey. [Wellesley, Mass.] Center for Research on Women, Wellesley Colelge, 1993. 26 p.

LRSD93-11907

"Over 4,200 girls returned surveys. Girls completing the surveys were in grades 2 through 12, and ranged in age from 9 to 19 years."

Yaffe, Elaine.

Expensive, illegal, and wrong: sexual harassment in our schools. Phi Delta Kappan, v. 77, Nov. 1995: K1-K15.

LRS95-13292

A Kappan special report. It discusses the history of sexual harassment in schools as well as some of the legal cases.

IV. THE LAW AND LEGAL CASES

Adler, Robert S. Pierce, Ellen R

The legal, ethical and social implications of the "reasonable woman" standard in sexual harassment cases. Fordham law review, v. 61, Mar. 1993: 773-827.

LRS93-1920

Article examines "the development and implications of the 'reasonable woman' standard that is gaining increasing acceptance as the appropriate gauge for measuring the offensiveness of the conduct at issue in sexual harassment cases."

Bass, Stuart L.

Recent court decisions expand role of arbitration in harassment and other title VII cases. Labor law journal, v. 46, Jan. 1995: 38-47.

LRS95-506

Article concludes that recent court decisions signal "a trend by the courts toward the enforcement of such arbitration agreements, particularly in non-union situations."

Conlon, Kevin. Voigt, Catherine.

Sexual harassment: an American judicial perspective. Labor law journal, v. 111, Jan. 1997: 41-49.

LRS97-391

"This article will provide a judicial perspective on the sexual harassment liability of private employees by summarizing legal precedent, statutes, and social developments that have influenced the current judicial stance on sexual harassment. Finally, the article will discuss methods employers are using to protect themselves from liability in light of judicial decisions pertaining to sexual harassment."

Conn, Jennifer L.

Sex harassment: a Thirteenth Amendment response. Columbia journal of law and social problems, v. 28, summer 1995: 519-557.

LRS95-7433

Comment "suggests that the First Amendment problems yet to be confronted are not insurmountable. Despite Title VII's restrictions on sexually harassing speech, Congress has the power to enact such restrictions through its Thirteenth Amendment mandate to abolish all badges and incidents of slavery. The victims of sexual harassment are in a similar position of the female slaves of the 1800s. To a large extent, today's economy makes employment a necessity, and mobility between jobs is difficult, if not impossible. The Thirteenth Amendment, although adopted expressly to outlaw black slavery, is equally a protections for all."

Cooper, Stacy J.

Sexual harassment and the Swedish Bikini Team: a reevaluation of the "hostile environment" doctrine. Columbia journal of law and social problems, v. 26, spring 1993: 387-434.

LRS93-6728

"The Swedish Bikini Team appeared in television commercials for Old Milwaukee Beer, a product of the Stroh Brewery Company. The advertising campaign is now the subject of a sexual harassment lawsuit filed by several [St. Paul] Stroh factory workers. The Author describes the development of sexual harassment law and analyzes the dispute over the appropriate standard for deciding when a working environment is hostile. The Author also discusses the extent to which the First Amendment prevents the regulation of sexist speech."

Current issues in sexual harassment law. Vanderbilt law review, v. 48, May 1995: 1009-1214.

LRS95-7655

Contents.—The forgotten interest group: reforming title VII to address the concerns of workers while eliminating sexual harassment.—Using agency principles for guidance in finding employer liability for a supervisor's hostile work environment sexual harassment.—Hooters: should there be an assumption of risk defense to some hostile work environment sexual harassment claims?—Proving welcomeness: the admissibility of evidence of sexual history in sexual harassment claims under the 1994 amendments to Federal Rule of Evidence 412.

Dale, Charles V.

Sexual harassment: a history of federal law. May 7, 1993. Washington, Congressional Research Service, 1993. 17 p.

93-495 A

Basically, the federal law of sexual harassment has evolved over a period of nearly two decades as the result of lower federal court decisions and U.S. Supreme Court precedent, interpreting the sex discrimination prohibition in Title VII of the 1964 Civil Rights Act and related federal law. Two forms of sexual harassment are forbidden by current Title VII caselaw and administrative guidelines issued by the Equal Employment Opportunity Commission (EEOC).

Sexual harassment and violence against women: developments in federal law. Oct. 18, 1996. Wahsington, Congressional Research Service, 1996, 27 p.

96-862 A

This report traces the statutory and judicial development of federal law in relation to sexual harassment and violence against women.

Hadley, Ernest C. Chuzi, George M.

Sexual harassment: federal law. Arlington, Va., Dewey Publications, C1995. 251 p.

KF3467.H33 1995

Partial contents.—Defining sexual harassment.—Quid pro quo harassment.—Hostile environment harassment.—Liability for sexual harassment.—Procedures and remedies.

Hames, David S.

Examining the relationship between Title VII's sexual harassment prohibitions and the First Amendment's free speech provisions: is there a conflict? Labor law journal, v. 46, Mar. 1995: 175-181.

LRS95-2104

"The purpose of this investigation is to clarify the relationship between he First Amendment's guarantee of freedom of speech and Title VII's sexual harassment prohibitions. More specifically, it will identify the circumstances in which employees' complaints or protestations against sexual harassment are protected by the First Amendment's free speech provisions. Relevant court decisions rendered throughout the United States will be examined to accomplish these objectives."

Jones, Constance.

Sexual harassment. New York, Facts on File, c1996. 280 p. (Library in a book)

HQ1237.5.U6J66 1996

Partial contents.—The Law of sexual harassment.—Organizations and agencies.—EEOC guidelines on sexual harassment, from the 1990 Guidelines on Discrimination Because of Sex.—Title IX of the 1972 Education Amendments.

Karner, Jessica M.

Political speech, sexual harassment, and a captive workforce. California law review, v. 83, Mar. 1995: 637-691.

LRS95-13687

"The author argues that harassing speech in the workplace should be regulable when it infringes greatly on the captive listener and contributes little to self-governance. Consistent with this rationale, this Comment argues that the captive audience doctrine, traditionally applied only in the home, should be expanded into the workforce."

Korn, Jane Byeff.

The fungible woman and other myths of sexual harassment. Tulane law review, v. 67, May 1993: 1363-1419.

LRS93-7307

Article "describes a legal regime driven by cultural stereotypes that ignores the gendered nature of sexual harassment. The article focuses on decisions treating workers' compensation as the exclusive state-law remedy for sexual harassment. Professor Korn suggeests that such treatment is flawed."

Lewis, Darryll M. Halcomb.

Sexual harassment under workers' compensation law. Labor law journal, v. 44, May 1993: 297-306.

LRS93-3904

"This paper explores the judicial treatment of sexual harassment under workers' compensation laws. It recommends that states statutorily exclude workers' compensation claims arising out of sexual harassment. The paper discusses recent cases which have held that sexual harassment claims are not covered by workers' compensation, thus recognizing that many jurisdictions have judicially achieved the result advanced in this paper."

Marcosson, Samuel A.

Harassment on the basis of sexual orientation: a claim of sex discrimination under Title VII. Georgetown law journal, v. 81, Nov. 1992:1-38.

LRS92-10758

"In Part I, I briefly describe the treatment of sexual orientation generally under Title VII, and explain why the traditional view that Title VII does not bar discrimination against gay men and lesbians is wrong. Even assuming, however, that discrimination against homosexuals generally is not covered by Title VII, I proceed in Part II to argue that the specific case of sexual orientation harassment is different, and gay men and lesbians are protected from this sort of discrimination."

Marcus,. Erig H.

Sexual harassment claims: who is a reasonable woman? Labor law journal, v. 44, Oct. 1993: 646-649.

LRS93-11148

Defines the "reasonable woman" standard in judging sexual harassment litigation.

McDonald, James J., Jr. Lees-Haley, Paul R.

Avoiding "junk science" in sexual harassment litigation. Employee relations law journal, v, 21, autumn 1995: 51-71.

LRS95-8765

"An increasing number of sexual harassment plaintiffs are seeking to recover substantial damages for psychological injuries. Many such plaintiffs rely on expert testimony from mental health professionals that often amounts to little more than 'junk science' and conjecture....Expert opinions based solely on the expert's clinical skills and experience may similarly be inadmissible if the expert lacks the requisite training, lacks prior experience with similar cases, or fails to follow commonly accepted diagnostic protocols."

McGurie, Powers.

Harris v. Forklift Systems, Inc. and hostile work environment harassment. Labor law journal, v. 46. May 1995: 314-320

LRS95-4233

Article discusses a Supreme Court case on sexual harassment and "outlines some of the requirements for proving a claim of sexual harassment under Title VII" of the Civil Rights Act.

Perry, Sarah H.

Enough is enough: per se constructive discharge for victims of sexually hostile work environments under Title VII. Washington law review, v. 70, Apr. 1995: 541-561.

LRS95-6221

"This Comment addresses the problems encountered by Jane and other victims of sexual harassment who quit their jobs in response to a hostile and abusive work environment..., highlights the inappropriateness of the current approaches to constructive discharge in the hostile environment context, and proposes a rule that would necessitate a finding of constructive discharge when a court finds a sexually hostile work environment...Argues that the proposed rule is fair, promotes the purposes of Title VII, and is supported by public policy."

Peterson, Donald J.

Individual liability of supervisors for acts of sexual harassment. Labor law journal, v. 47, Jan. 1996: 25-31.

LRS96-550

Article says that "when a supervisor uses the cloak of authority granted to him by the employer to elicit sexual favors, the employer must assume the liability for the acts of its management...What is not clear in the law is whether or not the victim of sexual harassment can also name, and make liable for damages, supervisors, as well as the defendant employer. It is the purpose of this paper to review federal court decisions to determine the current status of this important issue."

Piskorski, Thomas J.

Reinstatement of the sexual harasser: the conflict between federal labor law and Title VII. Employee relations law journal, v. 18, spring 1993: 617-623.

LRS93-721

Article states that "for a variety of reasons, arbitrators may decide that a lesser form of discipline than that imposed by the employer is warranted for acts of sexual harassment. This article will address the several federal courts of appeals' decisions that have attempted to resolve this conflict."

Roszkiowski, Christie L. Wayland, Robert F.

Arbitration review: is the public policy against sexual harassment sufficient cause for vacating an arbitration award? Labor law journal, v. 44, Nov. 1993: 707-716.

LRS93-10903

Article reviews the Stroehmann Bakeries case which "reviewed an arbitration award reinstating an employee accused of committing sexual harassment. This case illustrates the confluence of several important policies: judicial deferral to arbitrator's decisions in cases involving application and interpretation of collective bargaining agreements, the judicial refusal to enforce arbitration awards that violate public policy, and the public against sexual harassment in the workplace."

Sex discrimination: employment discrimination prohibited by Title VII of the Civil Rights Act of 1964, as amended, and the Equal Pay Act of 1963. Washington, U.S.
Equal Employment Opportunity Commission, 1995. 1 v. in various pagings

LRS95-10805

Partial contents.—Recognizing, correcting, and preventing sexual harassment.—EEOC fact sheets—sexual harassment.—29 CFR Part 1604 guidelines on discrimination because of sex.—EEOC notice March 3, 1990 policy guidance on current issues of sexual harassment.—The "reasonable person" standard: Harris v. Forklift Systems, Inc.—EEOC fact sheet—the Pregnancy Discrimination Act.

Terpstra, David E.

The process and outcomes of sexual harassment claims. Labor law journal, v. 44, Oct. 193: 632-638.

LRS93-11149

"This article will provide a general description of the process involved in filing formal charges of sexual harassment. Information will also be presented regarding the outcomes or odds of winning a case. Additionally, some of the case variables or factors that appear to influence the outcomes of sexual harassment charges will be identified and discussed."

Volokh, Eugene.

Freedom of speech and appellate review in workplace harassment cases. Northwestern University law review, v. 90, spring 1996: 1009-1031.

LRS96-6605

"Though there's a hot debate over whether and to what extent [harassing] speech restriction is constitutional, for this Article I'll set that question aside. I'll assume that, like obscenity, fighting words, and defamation, harassing speech—speech that creates a hostile environment—may constitutionally be restricted. Given this assumption, I'll argue, it's especially important that courts define the boundaries of this category as precisely as possible. And this sort of definition can happen only if courts exercise independent judgment in reviewing findings of a hostile environment."

Wanner, Barbara.

Mitsubishi Motors' sexual harassment case: were Japanese culture, management practices to blame? Washington, Japan Economic Institute, 1996. [18] p. (JEI report no. 26A)

LRS96-4261

Traces the development of a sexual harassment lawsuit filed by the Equal Employment Opportunity Commission against Mitsubishi Motors Management of America, Inc. "The prevailing view in many business circles is that MMMA's response to the EEOC suit may represent the best example to date of how a company should not manage a crisis."

Watson, Jerome R.

Employer liability for the sexually harassing actions of its customers. Employee relations law journal, v. 19, winter 1993-94: 227-237.

LRS93-11376

Article concludes that "employer liability for the sexually harassing actions of nonemployees is a harsh remedy to impose on employers, and though rarely addressed, courts recognize this fact. It has generally been in those situations where the employer has been insensitive to the harassment, failed to address it, or, due to its actions, virtually encouraged it that the employer has been held liable."

Zachery, Mary-Kathryn.

From construction to cases: the emergence of the obnoxious employee defense. Labor law journal, v. 47, Mar. 1996: 183-198

LRS96-1518

"This article will briefly review the history of sexual harassment law under Title VII of the Civil Rights Act of 1964, outline the relevant controversy about its interpretation, discuss the cases using the obnoxious employee defense, and finally offer observations on these cases."

INDEX

F

G

H

I

J

L

M

N

U

V

W